BAN...

THE...

Royal Bang...
Best seen fr...
inherited pri...
tenements. A horse-racing track encircles
Thailand's first golf course, opened in 1906.

All Seasons Place
The centrepiece of this cluster of skyscrapers
is the 210m CRC Tower, which was completed
in 2001 but looks straight out of the 1980s,
with its blue glass and jumbled geometries.
87 Thanon Witthayu

Lumphini Park
Originally royal property, it was opened to the
public in the 1920s. Locals play backgammon,
under pagodas, and *takraw* (kick volleyball).

Dusit Thani
Unbelievably, this was once Bangkok's tallest
building. Its blend of modern architecture and
Thai elements, including a slim gold spire, still
make it one of the city's most distinguished.
See p087

Abdulrahim Place
Interdesign Co's mash-up of postmodern and
Gotham styles was finished in 1997. Its golden
pyramid riffs with the Dusit Thani next door.
990 Thanon Rama IV

Q-House Lumphini
More blue glass envelops this surreal take on
a medieval fortress, inspired by Thai motifs.
The buttresses and crown light up at night.
1 Thanon Sathorn Tai

Thai Wah Tower II
Head to the top of this slender 1995 pomo
tower, replete with void, for the alfresco bar
(see p065), unbeatable for a sundowner.
21/100 Thanon Sathorn Tai

INTRODUCTION
THE CHANGING FACE OF THE URBAN SCENE

There's a media-fed familiarity to Bangkok, a coruscant whirl that takes in floating fruit markets, street vendors' sizzling hotplates and Buddhist stupas overlooking red-light districts. It's a contradictory mix of new money and no money – luxury condos and malls share area codes with tumbledown slums, and a modern transport system coexists with crammed water taxis. These economic fault lines are partly to blame for past unrest, as a comfortable, educated urban population is pitted against the steady flow of rural poor who come to the capital in search of work. In 2016, the death of revered King Bhumibol Adulyadej, who was widely seen as a unifying force, was not unexpected, but was nonetheless deeply felt. Thai politics have steadied under the military-led government that came to power in a bloodless coup in 2014, but for how long is anyone's guess, and flux is the continuing theme of this resilient city.

Today's Bangkok smacks of sophistication – the Calatrava-style Rama VIII Bridge, the citywide planting of trees, even the tuk-tuks run on liquid propane. A swathe of chic new restaurants justifies its status as an Asian food hub, and you can swill mojitos in five-star bars, trying to pick out the *hi-so* (high society) from the wannabes. You can still do old-school Bangkok too, living out hard-boiled noir subplots, ambling through riverside alleys and ogling scorpions at the market. It is your call, and the frisson produced by this choice is what makes Bangkok the beguiling temptress that she is.

ESSENTIAL INFO
FACTS, FIGURES AND USEFUL ADDRESSES

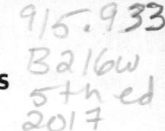

915.933
B216w
5th ed
2017

TOURIST OFFICE
Tourism Authority of Thailand
1600 Thanon Petchaburi Mai
T 02 250 5500
www.tourismthailand.org

TRANSPORT
Airport transfer to city centre
www.srtet.co.th
Trains depart regularly, from 6am to midnight. The journey takes 30 minutes
BTS Skytrain
T 02 617 7300
www.bts.co.th
MRT metro
T 02 624 5200
www.bemplc.co.th
All trains run from 6am to midnight
Taxis
Siam Taxi
T 1661
Cabs can be hailed on the street. Ask to have the meter turned on

EMERGENCY SERVICES
Emergencies
T 191
Tourist police
T 1155
24-hour pharmacy
Foodland Supermarket Pharmacy
48 Column Tower, Sukhumvit Soi 16

EMBASSIES
British Embassy
14 Thanon Witthayu
T 02 305 8333
www.gov.uk/government/world/thailand
US Embassy
95 Thanon Witthayu
T 02 205 4000
th.usembassy.gov

POSTAL SERVICES
Post office
Thanon Khaosan
Soi Damnoen Klang Nua
Shipping
DHL Express
The Old Siam
50 Thanon Tri Phet

BOOKS
Architects 49 Ltd: Selected and Current Works edited by Kate Ryan and Eliza Hope (Images Publishing)
Classic Thai: Design Interiors Architecture by Chami Jotisalikorn, Phuthorn Bhumadhon and Virginia McKeen Di Crocco (Tuttle Publishing)

WEBSITES
Art
www.mocabangkok.com
Newspaper
www.bangkokpost.com

EVENTS
International Festival of Dance & Music
www.bangkokfestivals.com
Thailand International Furniture Fair
www.thailandfurniturefair.com

COST OF LIVING
Taxi from Suvarnabhumi International Airport to city centre
THB450
Cappuccino
THB100
Packet of cigarettes
THB110
Daily newspaper
THB30
Bottle of champagne
THB3,000

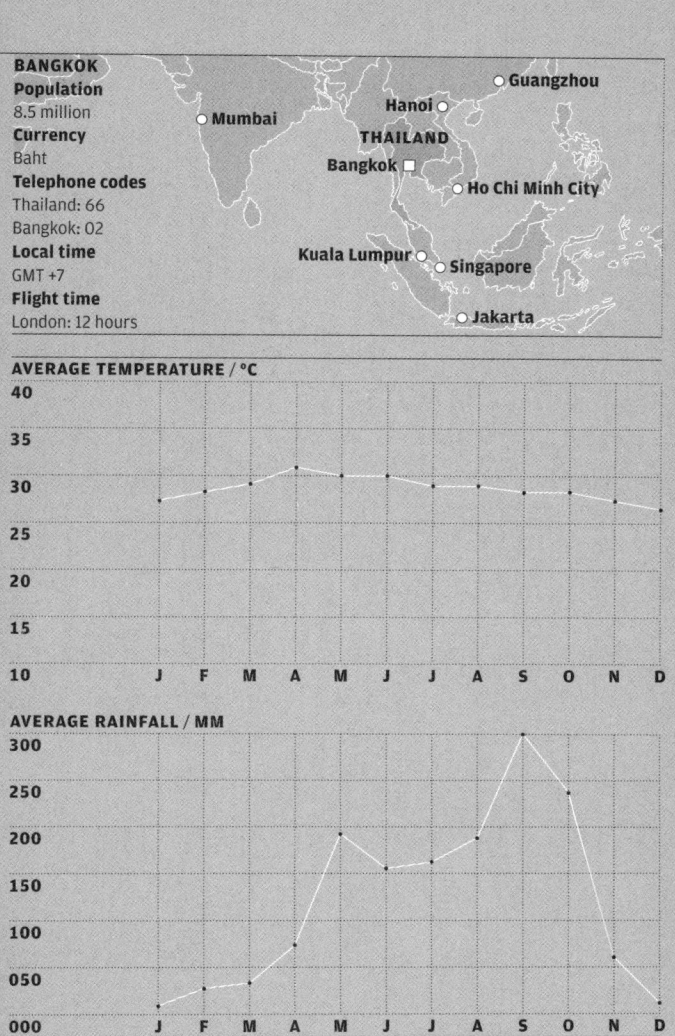

NEIGHBOURHOODS
THE AREAS YOU NEED TO KNOW AND WHY

To help you navigate the city, we've chosen the most interesting districts (see below and the map inside the back cover) and colour-coded our featured venues, according to their location; those venues that are outside these areas are not coloured.

CHATUCHAK
In the north of the city, the wooden sprawl of the world-famous Chatuchak Weekend Market (or 'JJ') is on the edge of the little-known Chatuchak Park. Whisking you out here are the Skytrain and MRT, the latter more convenient for the market. Nearby, you'll also find one of the best selections of fresh produce in Bangkok, at the Or Tor Kor Market (Thanon Kamphaeng Phet), and vibrant, if off-the-radar, nightlife.

OLD TOWN/BANGLUMPHU
Where the wide lanes of Thanon Sathorn reach the nut-brown Chao Phraya, hotels rise up with imperious garishness. To the north, wooden architecture and noodle vendors mark the de facto Old Town. It is a mix of ancient and modern, from hidden Hokkien coffee shops to style boutiques. In Banglamphu, bustling Thanon Phra Athit is lined with shophouses and live-music bars. Avoid the traffic by catching a ferry here from Saphan Taksin pier in Sathorn.

SUKHUMVIT
This traffic-clogged, mall-laden avenue goes on and on for miles. It contains plenty of happening sub-sections, whether that be leafy lanes like Soi 31, with its furniture and fashion studios, or hip enclaves such as Thonglor (Soi 55) and Ekkamai (Soi 63), all neighbourhoods unto themselves. Many eating, drinking and dancing hotspots are found around here, including Shugaa (see p049) and Quince (see p058).

RATCHAPRASONG
Students, high-haired society wives and models flock to this shopping and youth-culture hub. They flow between the air-con malls on Thanons Rama I and Ploenchit, from Siam Discovery (see p089) to Central Embassy (see p013). In the backstreets you will find the 1969 Scala Film Theatre (Siam Square Soi 2), a gem by architect Chira Silpakanok that melds art deco with Thai modernism, with a glorious vaulted lobby.

SILOM/SATHORN
South-west of the green lung of Lumphini Park is a line of skyscrapers, including the idiosyncratic Robot Building (see p085) and the soaring MahaNakhon Tower (see p012). The heart of the district is Thanon Silom and cross streets Convent and Saladaeng. A series of minor thoroughfares are lined with gay bars, dance halls, cabarets and fine restaurants, from Eat Me (Soi Pipat 2, T 02 238 0391) to Le Du (399/3 Silom Soi 7, T 092 919 9969) and Bunker (see p046).

ARI
Located between the Victory Monument and Chatuchak, Ari is one of the city's most chilled neighbourhoods. Low-rise and with a villagey vibe, it's home to families, young professionals and an expat community. Along its sun-dappled laneways you will find tempting street food stalls, a slew of third-wave coffee shops, hip bars and club spaces like Future Factory (see p070), and inventive fusion restaurant Salt (see p064).

LANDMARKS
THE SHAPE OF THE CITY SKYLINE

Bangkok is a textbook example of urban Asian sprawl. It has many multi-lane highways in the wrong parts of town and bottlenecked single-lane avenues in the right ones. But with good planning, it can be split into work, shop and play zones and managed accordingly.

Retail outlets are mainly concentrated on one long, smoggy drag that begins by Siam Square and unfurls east, past the 2014 Central Embassy (see p013), joining Thanon Sukhumvit near seedy Nana Plaza. Sukhumvit's *sois* (side lanes) are like mini-neighbourhoods; key streets are Soi 63, or Ekkamai, hub of the party scene; Soi 55, aka Thonglor, home to high-end malls like J Avenue (No 15); and Soi 11, which offers a complete night out on one strip.

The 2001 State Tower (1055 Thanon Silom), a 247m landmark by Thai architects Rangsan, marks the southern boundary of the Old Town. Here, alleys lined with wooden shophouses lead to the Wat Pho (2 Thanon Sanamchai) temple and Royal Grand Palace (Thanon Na Phra Lan), set by the banks of the Chao Phraya, once the city's lifeblood and still a major artery. The other areas to visit are Silom and Sathorn, a hotchpotch of offices, swish hotels, A-list haunts, and the sleaze of Patpong. Above all of this now soars the impressive MahaNakhon Tower (see p012), which usurped the 1997 Baiyoke Tower II (222 Soi Ratchaprarop 3) as king of the Bangkok skyline in 2016, but is just one spike in a multi-pronged assault.
For full addresses, see Resources.

CAT Building

The customer service nerve centre of CAT Telecom, this 31-floor tower sits on the Chao Phraya, from where it beams radio waves across the city. It's the kind of lumpen, glass-and-steel brute that gives new Asian architecture such a bad name, but does make a useful reference point along the river; likewise, the dome of the State Tower (pictured, right).
72 Thanon Charoen Krung

MahaNakhon Tower

Even in a city with 12 (and counting) towers higher than 200m, MahaNakhon ('Great Metropolis') makes quite a statement. At 314m, it claimed the title of tallest building in Thailand in 2016, albeit briefly, as the Magnolias Waterfront Residences (215 Thanon Charoen Nakorn) is set to pip it in 2018. But most striking is its design by Ole Scheeren/OMA. A wave of 'pixels' (stepped boxy recesses that house terraces and balconies) corkscrews around the facade, counteracting its immense scale. According to Scheeren, it reflects Bangkok's intensity and energy: 'In some ways, it almost seems unfinished,' he said. Inside are restaurants, retail, the buzzy Edition hotel (see p016), 200 condos and an observation deck and bar on levels 74 to 75 with a glass-encased walkway that cantilevers out into the air.
114 Thanon Narathiwat, T 02 234 1414

Central Embassy

Bangkok's most opulent lifestyle hub cost more than £400m to build. Constructed on the former gardens of the British Embassy, it encompasses a luxury mall and a Park Hyatt, hosts exhibitions, fashion shows and glitzy events, and marks the eastern end of a run of shopping experiences that includes CentralWorld and Siam Paragon. London architects Amanda Levete tied it all together with a facade of ribbon glass and aluminium shingles, inspired by classic Thai patterns, which envelops both the six-level retail podium and the 27-storey hotel tower above, giving it a shimmer that glints in the sun, while its sinuous curves and racing-stripe design call to mind the work of Zaha Hadid. Inside, check out the outlet of local fashion brand Disaya (see p094) and Eathai, an upscale street-food court.
1031 Thanon Ploenchit, T 02 119 7777

Elephant Tower
A testament to locals' affinity to all that's eye-popping, the 1997 Elephant Tower, brainchild of real estate and engineering mogul Arun Chaiseri and the architect Ongard Satrabhandhu, would not have worked in any other capital. Its leg-like pillars, pinkish-grey facade and cut-out eye might be gaudy, but somehow, in a Thai context, have a camp, quirky appeal.
369/38 Thanon Phahon Yothin 26

HOTELS
WHERE TO STAY AND WHICH ROOMS TO BOOK

If there is any single business that benefits from the no worries/all smiles Thai approach to life and the fluid grace of Buddhist society, it is hospitality. First-time visitors to Bangkok are often drawn to the tranquillity of the river, where colonial-style five-star choices with impressive views are plentiful, from the grande dame Mandarin Oriental (48 Charoen Krung Soi 38, T 02 659 9000) to the opulent Shangri-La (see p031). Other Chao Phraya options are The Peninsula (333 Thanon Charoen Nakhon, T 02 020 2888) and Millennium Hilton (123 Thanon Charoen Nakhon, T 02 442 2000). For a more intimate experience, try Arun Residence (see p022).

Downtown, there has been a trend towards design-conscious refits, such as at Hotel Muse (55/555 Soi Lang Suan, T 02 630 4000), where interiors are a mash-up of the golden King Rama V era and fin-de-siècle elegance, and Luxx XL (82/8 Soi Lang Suan, T 02 684 1111), a 50-room conversion of a seven-storey building that managed to create enough room for a 12m infinity pool. Elsewhere, a sluggish economy has not halted the arrival of several flash new hotels. The Park Hyatt (T 02 012 1234) opened in Central Embassy (see p013) in 2017, and features a series of leafy outdoor terraces, and decor by Yabu Pushelberg. In 2018, the MahaNakhon Tower (see p012) will house a 150-room Edition (T 02 055 1414) on the first 18 floors, a hip, splashy collaboration between Ian Schrager and Marriott. *For full addresses and room rates, see Resources.*

LiT
This offbeat new-build injected a shot of design into an unremarkable section of downtown in 2011. Conceived by VaSLab (see p100), the L-shaped property has a detached facade, or 'veil', of laser-cut aluminium that creates an interplay of light and shade. The public spaces are set over two levels, and consist of a garden, a spiralling staircase to the pool, beneath which is a bijou spa, and an outdoor bar, leading to the restaurant. The 79 rooms are rather run-of-the-mill but perfectly functional, enhanced by darkwood floors, statement walls and curtained-off tubs, and are popular with the *hi-so* crowd. A tuk-tuk shuttles guests to the Skytrain, and a series of elevated walkways connect to nearby hubs like the BACC (see p037). *36/1 Soi Kasemsan, Thanon Rama I, T 02 612 3456, www.litbangkok.com*

Sala Rattanakosin
Superbly situated opposite Wat Arun (see p045), this 15-room hotel was converted from a row of traditional shophouses. Local firm Onion preserved the original features, such as the exposed brickwork, and melded them with gold laminated glass, aluminium panels and sculptural elements, like a cubed, black powder-coated metal chandelier in reception. Sala's often billed as a 'restaurant with rooms', so it's not surprising that dining is a highlight here, due to English chef Tony Wrigley's classic Thai cooking. Not that the rooms are disappointing; check in to one with views of the Chao Phraya, such as the River View Deluxe (pictured). Alternatively, head to the sleek rooftop bar for a 360-degree skyline panorama. *39 Thanon Maharat, T 02 622 1388, www.salaresorts.com/rattanakosin*

Yim Huai Khwang

Located away from the centre but with easy MRT access, this upscale hostel is a stylish budget option. Yim means 'smile', and there's a cheerfulness to the service, and to local firm Supermachine's design. The public areas are a riot of colour, from the turquoise and citrus-hued stairwell (opposite) to the marble reception, which is plastered with magazine clippings. The lobby (above) doubles as a hip café. The communal dwellings have a Japanese feel, with bunks set in capsule-like units. But we recommend you reserve one of the private rooms; the Double Bed Garden opens out onto nature and bamboo. On-site dining is basic, but the Huai Khwang area is great for street food, and if you'd rather sit down, Noi Seafood (T 02 692 7439) is legendary.
*70 Thanon Pracha Rat Bamphen,
T 080 965 9994, www.yimbangkok.com*

Arun Residence
Portuguese colonial-style architecture coexists with Ratanakosin-era and more modern art at this boutique hotel. The overhaul of a waterfront warehouse was overseen by Thai architect and interior designer Chavalit Chavawan, who created a simply decorated, two-storey, seven-room hideaway by the Chao Phraya river. We suggest you plump for the spacious Arun Suite (right). Rooms that lack air-conditioning can get rather stuffy, but this only adds to the authentic ambience; the hotel is located in a fascinating lane filled with numerous shophouses selling everything from metal panelling to rice. The breathtaking views of Wat Arun (see p045) are best enjoyed at sunrise and at dusk, while enjoying Thai fusion cuisine at The Deck restaurant on Arun's veranda.
36-38 Soi Pratoo Nok Yoong,
Thanon Maharat, T 02 221 9158,
www.arunresidence.com

HOTELS

The Siam
Bangkok has a deeply ingrained penchant for riverside living, and the delightful The Siam, on a 1.2-hectare plot north of the Rama VIII Bridge, expanded the city's fine selection back in 2012. Owner Krissada Sukosol Clapp is known locally for his pop music and film roles, but on show here is his impressive collection of antiques and curios – including everything from dentist chairs to French horns suspended above the chequered tiles of the dapper Deco Bar & Bistro. Architect and designer Bill Bensley has introduced muted tones with art deco-style furnishings, as evidenced in the public spaces (above). Each of the 39 suites and pool villas, either set around the breezy atrium (opposite) or frangipani-shaded courtyards, is serviced by a butler.
3/2 Thanon Khao, T 02 206 6999, www.thesiamhotel.com

The Cabochon Hotel
Although the interiors of this four-suite, four-studio hotel may appear convincingly aged, it actually only opened its doors in 2012. Propelling the city's current trend for boutique properties with period aesthetics, owner and interior designer Eugene Yeh has paid extraordinary attention to detail to immerse guests in a time capsule of 1920s Shanghai; a place where filmmaker Wong Kar-Wai's imagination might roam.

Vanity mirrors are set in antique wooden frames, the bedheads are plush, and the suites (above) have spacious living rooms. The commitment to authenticity continues at the Joy Luck Salon de Thé, the lounge and cocktail bar, which is filled with models of classic airplanes, vintage Louis Vuitton steamer trunks and a dusty set of books.
14/29 Sukhumvit Soi 45, T 02 259 2871, www.cabochonhotel.com

Siam Kempinski Hotel
Opened in 2010, this 401-room city resort sits on land that was formerly part of the neighbouring Sra Pathum Palace, current home of Princess Maha Chakri Sirindhorn. The lotus is omnipresent throughout the property's eclectic interiors, provided by Hirsch Bedner Associates, and dominates a collection of arty photography in each guest bedroom. Local architects Tandem devised a horseshoe layout where all the accommodation looks out onto tropical landscaping and three saltwater pools; the gardens are unfeasibly quiet, given the Kempinski's proximity to the bustling Siam district. Suites feature a slick working area and luxe marble bathrooms. Dine at the modern Thai restaurant Sra Bua and chill at the poolside Rotunda bar (above).
991/9 Thanon Rama I, T 02 162 9000, www.kempinski.com/bangkok

SO Sofitel

Christian Lacroix provided the finishing touches to the quiff-like, 30-storey SO Sofitel, designed by Thai architect Smith Obayawat. Its 238 rooms and suites are based on the five elements; Water rooms have bathtubs with epic panoramas, and Woods (SO Lofty, pictured) feature teak-panelled walls. A glamorous 10th-floor infinity pool overlooks Lumphini Park.
2 Thanon Sathorn Nua, T 02 624 0000

Chakrabongse Villas
This urban retreat takes its name from a Thai prince, who commissioned these Ayutthaya-style stilted wooden villas for entertaining in the early 20th century. Rooms and suites, which include the Thai House, the Riverside Villa, the Chinese Suite and the Garden Suite (above), have an intimacy that evokes old European inns on a good day. Interiors feature luxurious beds, polished floors, darkwood fittings and traditional furnishings. Among the amenities are a 10m pool, a chef who goes to market daily and a private boat mooring. As at the Arun Residence (see p022), you can gaze at Wat Arun across the river and, unlike many five-star waterfront hotels, there's a real sense of engagement with the rituals and rhythms of Thai life.
396 Thanon Maharat, T 02 222 1290, www.chakrabongsevillas.com

Shangri-La Hotel

The 802-room Shangri-La, which opened in 1986 and was given a £37m makeover in 2010, has enough facilities to make you feel as if you need never leave. Indeed, many of its guests shuttle only between the hotel and their respective business meetings in the city. The accommodation, divided between two wings, is plush, well-equipped and very comfortable – we were taken with the vistas from the Speciality Suite, and all of the rooms feature local touches, such as silk and teak elements. The complex's dozen restaurants serve Thai, Cantonese, Italian and global fare, and there are three bars. Recuperate in the health club or the CHI spa, and take a dip in the swimming pools hidden among the manicured, if slightly twee, gardens.
89 Soi Wat Suan Plu, T 02 236 7777, www.shangri-la.com/bangkok

24 HOURS
SEE THE BEST OF THE CITY IN JUST ONE DAY

Two decades ago, Bangkok had fewer than 100 7-Eleven stores and not a public-transport system or multi-lane expressway in sight. The very thought of trying to see the city in 24 hours would send shudders through wide-eyed tourists and locals alike. The further reaches of Sukhumvit consisted of little more than a country road and some paddy fields, and even the shortish hop from Lumphini Park to Chinatown was a major undertaking. Things have changed. Now, as well as the old methods of transport, such as motorbikes and boats, there's the MRT, the Skytrain and an airport rail link that connects to BTS Phaya Thai station, high above the congestion.

The City of Angels is one of extremes and to explore it properly you should experience them all: on land and on water; from high society down to grass-roots level; and from the royal palaces to the dizzying, fume-filled streets. This means having fun and not forgetting to relax. If a boat ride down the Chao Phraya (see p045) doesn't do it, then a massage at Ruen-Nuad (42 Thanon Convent, T 02 632 2662), followed by drinks and dinner at a style-conscious hangout like Bunker (see p046), surely will. Hopefully you'll have longer than 24 hours in this absorbing place, in which case, use our itinerary here simply as a guide, and save the schlep to MOCA (see p042) for a full afternoon. After all, this is the land of *sanuk* (which loosely translates as 'fun') and *mai pen rai* ('don't worry').
For full addresses, see Resources.

09.00 Ink & Lion Café

Founders Adithep Pinijpinyo and Nongphan Tangtaweekul met in San Francisco and transported their love of its coffee culture back to Ekkamai. Beans are sourced from northern Thailand and internationally and roasted in-house in small batches. There's also espresso and slow drip, and pastries such as lemon tart and coconut cake. The concrete and whitewashed brick lend Ink & Lion an industrial aesthetic, the vintage furnishings include school benches from Japan, and there are rotating exhibitions. It's closed Wednesday to Friday, but more substantial fare is on offer nearby at health café Theera (T 090 506 2222), where we're partial to the salmon on gluten-free, house-made bread. For a proper Thai breakfast, head to Ekkamai Congee (T 086 705 1251) for the rice porridge with pork or egg.
1/7 Ekkamai Soi 2, T 091 559 0994

10.00 RMA Institute

One of Bangkok's most forward-thinking art institutions is named after director Piyatat Hemmatat's gran ('*ar-ma*'), who once owned the building. It often shows documentary work, traditionally not recognised as an artform here, so this is one of the few places in the city where you will find photography by luminaries including Cattleya Jaruthavee and Nipon Intarit, whose exhibition 'Som' was a study through colour of the country's fractious recent political climate. RMA also displays other mediums, such as the cinematic oil paintings by Nijsupa Nakaurai ('The Blue Cinema', pictured). The non-profit venture shares the space with garden cafè Gastro 1/6 (T 080 603 6421) and hosts screenings and recitals. *238 Sukhumvit Soi 22, Soi Sai Nampthip 2, T 02 663 0809, www.rmainstitute.net*

035

24 HOURS

11.00 Almeta
Though most people flock to Jim Thompson House (T 02 216 7368) in their blind, giddy rush to check silk-buying off the list, there are a few singular alternatives more closely aligned with current trends. Tucked away in a pretty two-storey house on a quiet street, Almeta has provided its bespoke service since 1992, and in a field generally seen as stuffy, has cultivated a reputation for creativity and innovation. Your choice of yarns, weaves, weights and more than 1,000 colours can normally be delivered within days. There is also a prêt-à-porter line in washable, printed and pre-crinkled silk; bed linen and fabric by the metre; and collaborations with star designers. Everything is handwoven and produced at its factory in Isaan in north-east Thailand.
20/3 Sukhumvit Soi 23, T 02 258 4227, www.almeta.com

11.45 Bangkok Art and Culture Centre

For a taste of contemporary Thai art and design, head to the publicly funded BACC. After many years of planning disputes and changes in government, the centre finally opened in 2008. But it was only in 2012, after success with some high-profile and well-attended exhibitions, that this 10-storey hub carved its niche in a city that can, at times, be creatively decentred. Designed by architect Robert Boughey, the building is reminiscent of the New York Guggenheim's corkscrewed interior, mixed with the familiarity of a shopping centre for the Bangkok audience. Inside, find everything from local handicrafts in modest artist-run shops on the lower levels to internationally acclaimed artworks in the exhibition halls on the top three floors.
939 Thanon Rama I, T 02 214 6630, www.bacc.or.th

12.45 Grand Postal Building

Bangkok's post office, designed by Mew Aphaiwong, was built from 1935 to 1940, when the country was ruled by a military dictator, hence the rationalist style and fascist nuances. Silpa Bhirasri's salmon-pink Garuda sculptures provide a little exterior ornamentation. It is now home to the Thailand Creative Design Centre (TCDC), which puts on eclectic shows.
1160 Thanon Charoen Krung

24 HOURS

13.30 The Never Ending Summer
Duangrit Bunnag's influence is writ large on Thai architecture. His bold minimalist designs for resorts such as X2 Kui Buri (see p102) are widely acclaimed, while his H1 mall in Bangkok, now sadly turned into apartments, inspired a slew of other low-rise projects. Nowhere is his approach more apparent than at The Jam Factory, a transformation of three disused factories into a coffeehouse, gallery, bookshop, his own firm's offices and restaurant The Never Ending Summer. The dining area is defined by the building's original features, from the beamed ceiling to roughly hewn walls, brickwork and paint splatters. Chefs in the glass kitchen prepare recipes from Bunnag's childhood, such as stir-fried lotus stems with shrimp paste and minced pork, and braised pork belly with duck eggs. The courtyard often hosts markets and gigs.
41/5 Thanon Charoen Nakhon,
T 02 861 0953

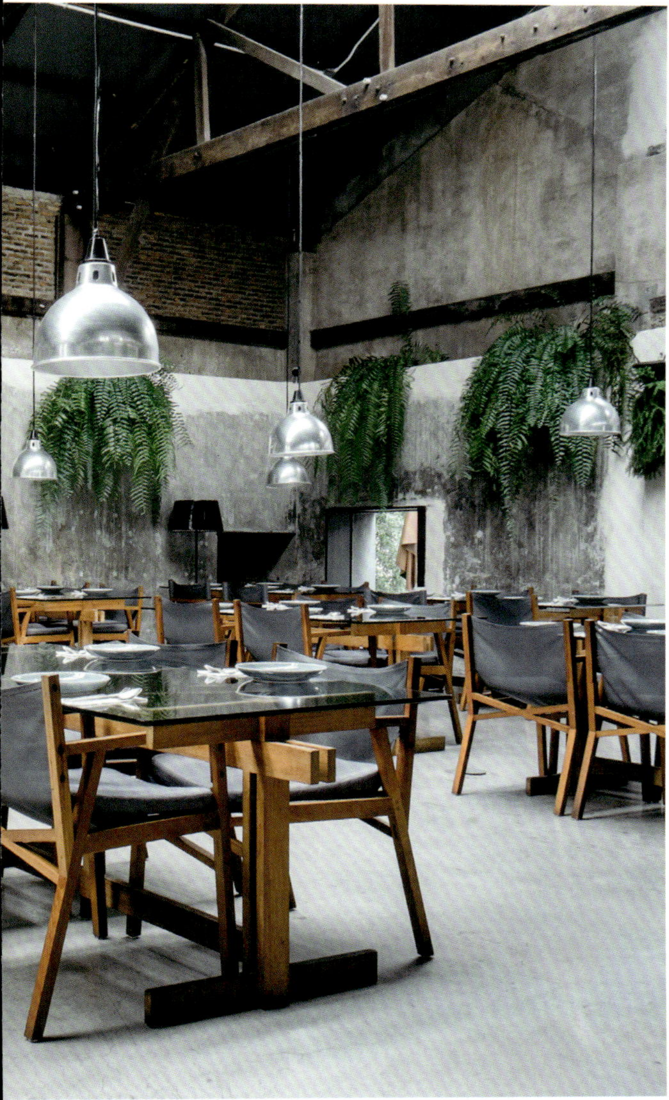

พิพิธภัณฑ์ศิลปะไทยร่วมสมัย
MOCA

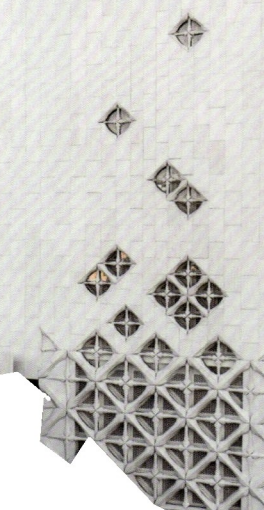

15.15 Museum of Contemporary Art
This extensive private collection is way up in the north but a trip here is essential. The museum was inaugurated in 2012 by tycoon Boonchai Bencharongkul to rotate the circa 800 pieces in his stash, as well as loans. The white cube is fronted by Nonthivathn Chandhanaphalin's *Happiness* sculpture (opposite) and its facade is perforated with openings in the form of cascading jasmine flowers. Inside is an overview of the Thai scene (paintings by Thawan Duchanee, above), since the late 1980s in particular. If you're short on time, don't miss Paitun Muangsomboon's hyper-realist sculptures and the gigantic 2011 triptych *The Three Kingdoms: Heaven, Middle Earth and Hell* by Sompop Butraj, Panya Wijinthanasan and Prateep Kochabua. Closed Mondays.
499 Thanon Kamphaengphet 6, Ladyao, T 02 016 5666, www.mocabangkok.com

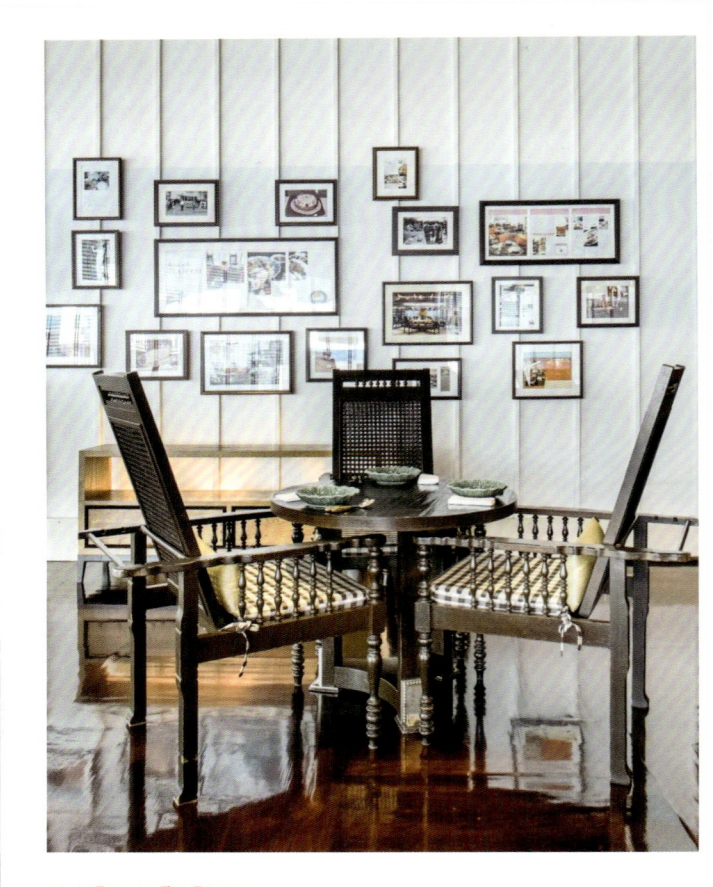

16.45 Erawan Tea Room

On the second floor of the Erawan mall, this tea room is a legendary venue dating back to the 1960s, where Jackie Kennedy is reputed to have dined. The interior, with its warm orange tones and contemporary Thai-Chinese detailing, was reinvented by designer Tony Chi. It's a pleasant place for a pitstop at any time of the day. It overlooks the Erawan Shrine, location of the tragic 2015 bombing, which the military regime cleared up in two days. The gilded statue here was erected in the 1950s to appease Lord Brahma during the construction of the Erawan Hotel, which subsequently became the Grand Hyatt (T 02 254 1234). Choose from Indian, Sri Lankan, Chinese or Thai varieties of tea, and if you like the brew, they are all packaged for take away. *494 Thanon Phloenchit, T 02 250 7777, www.erawanbangkok.com*

17.30 Wat Arun

The two different faces of Bangkok can be observed on the banks of the Chao Phraya, where Sino-Portuguese shophouses look across to gleaming, modern hotels. Take a river taxi from Saphan Taksin pier for the 15-minute ride to Tha Tien, past locals absent-mindedly fishing for their dinner. From here, an express boat will ferry you to the stucco-covered Wat Arun. Building work began during the Ayutthaya era (1350-1767), although the towering central prang, which is surrounded by four smaller ones, wasn't added until the 19th century. Wat Arun translates as the 'Temple of the Dawn', and earned its moniker from the manner in which light shimmers off its facade, which is decorated with porcelain that Chinese ships used as ballast before discarding. It is equally alluring at sunset.
34 Thanon Arun Amarin, T 02 891 2185

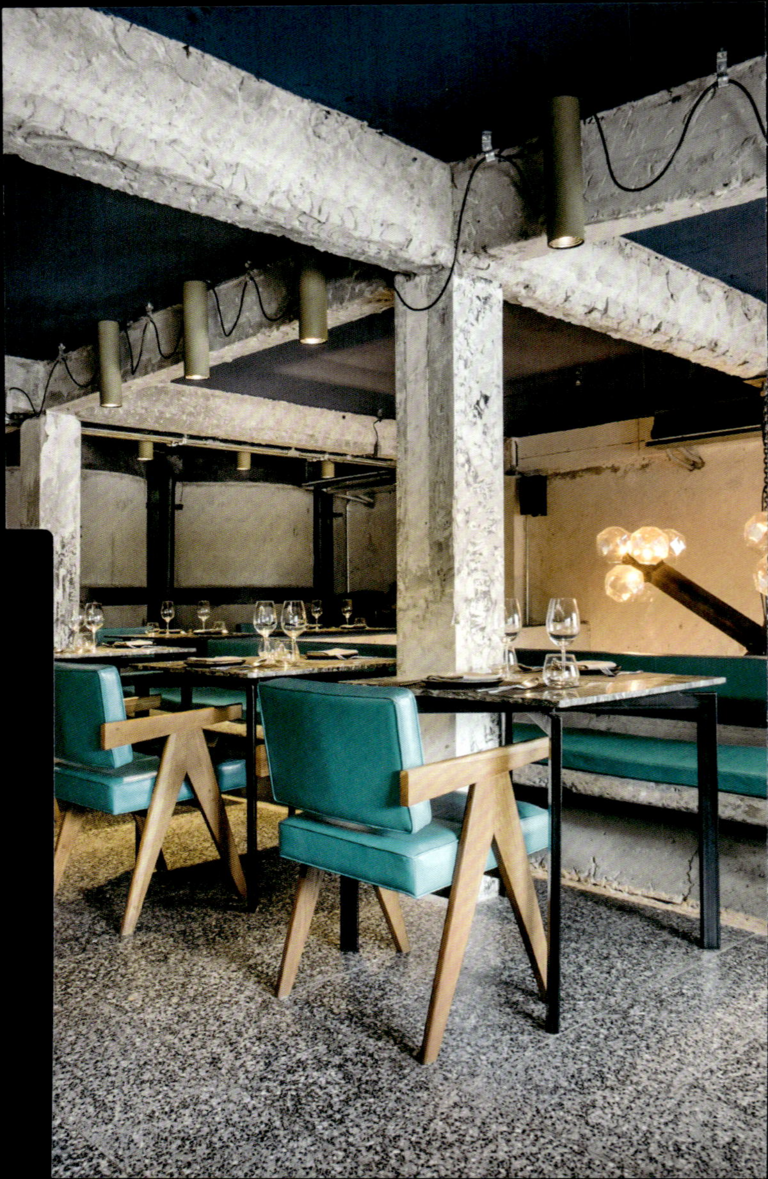

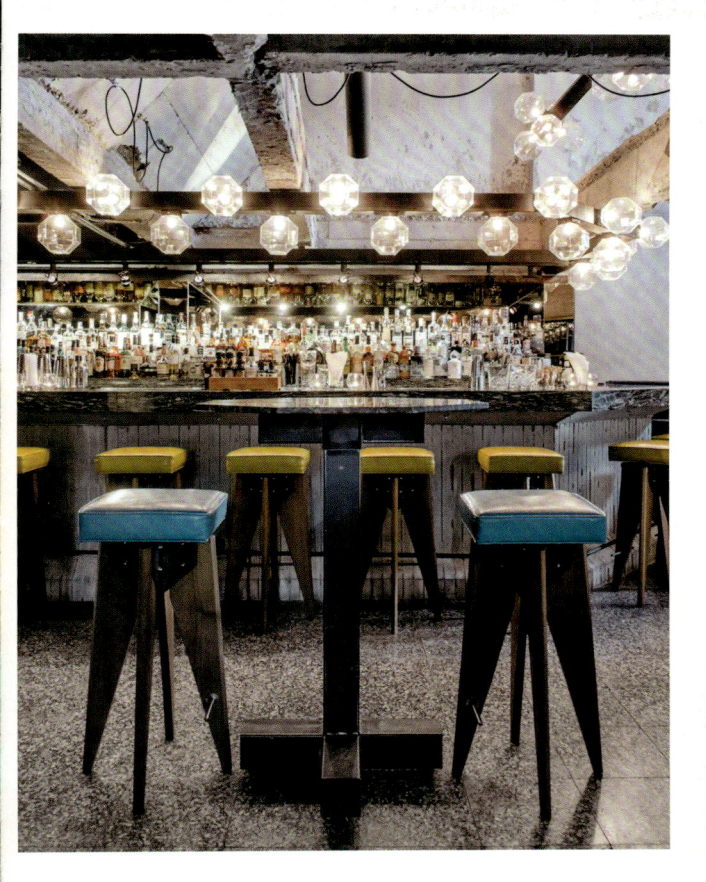

20.30 Bunker

Secreted away behind a brutal exterior is one of the city's most rewarding all-round dining experiences. The concept of refuge is key to the aesthetic. Kevin Lim of Lump Company Ltd and designer Kerry Wheatley have transformed the concrete shell of an old massage parlour, softening the bare walls and iron bracings with teak flooring, polished stone slabs, copper-toned mirrors and custom-made 'Octagon' pendant lights. Arnold Marcella, who perfected his craft at two-Michelin-starred Corton in New York, helms the kitchen and shows his pedigree in dishes such as beef tartare with soy sauce, fresh daikon and preserved quail egg, and Kanpachi sashimi with rhubarb and uni. His tender smoked Wagyu short ribs have reached near-legendary status. *118/2 Sathorn Soi 12, T 092 563 9991, www.bunkerbkk.com*

URBAN LIFE
CAFÉS, RESTAURANTS, BARS AND NIGHTCLUBS

Bangkok is Southeast Asia's most vibrant city in which to eat, drink, dance and all combinations thereof. There is superb food on nearly every street corner, and from these world-class hawkers offering grilled meat and noodles made *à la minute* to the raft of fine-diners such as Osha (see p052), the Thai capital is an epicurean paradise.

Nightlife can be broken down into various clusters. Westerners are drawn to lively Sukhumvit Soi 11, lined with eateries and party places. The European-style bars on Thanon Phra Athit are popular with locals, as are the upscale hotspots on Ekkamai and Thonglor, including mixology bar Rabbit Hole (125 Sukhumvit Soi 55, T 098 969 1335) and nightspot Beam (72 Sukhumvit Soi 55, T 02 392 7750). The clubs on Royal City Avenue (RCA) stay open late and blast out chart hits, while gay Bangkok centres on Silom Sois 2 and 4.

In Sathorn, Vesper (10/15 Thanon Convent, T 02 235 2777) mixes superb cocktails, while Smalls (186/3 Soi Suan Phlu 1, T 095 585 1398) entices with its 1960s townhouse setting, jazz soundtrack and rather dangerous selection of absinthe. Even more bohemian are the hangouts on and around Thanon Charoen Krung – Soulbar (No 954, T 093 220 0441), Teens of Thailand (see p053) and Tep Bar (see p057). Meanwhile, up-and-coming Ari has a villagey vibe. Soak it up at the Japanese fusion stalwart Pla Dib (1/1 Soi Ari Sampan 7, T 02 279 8185) and design-led venues such as Salt (see p064). *For full addresses, see Resources.*

Shugaa Dessert Bar

The decor of this concept café, devised by Thai studio Party/Space/Design, pays homage to its most obvious ingredient: sugar. The interiors – all creamy marble and pale wood – feature a palette of white, pistachio green, marshmallow and pastels. But most eyecatching are the polygon installation on the huge glass storefront, the sculptural burnt-sugar-coloured light fittings in the shape of sucrose molecules, and a spiral staircase with a crystal-like acrylic-box bannister. From the upstairs level, where pendants resemble oversized granules, there is a grandstand view of the pastry chefs in full flow. The desserts here have a Japanese influence, exemplified in creations such as the Kyotonite, which is made with *matcha*, caramelised almonds, red bean paste and green tea *mochi*.
27 Sukhumvit Soi 61, T 02 381 5940

Storyline

Architects Junsekino transformed part of a modern office building in bustling Phrom Phong into this chic co-working café. The floor area was extended with a teak-clad patio terrace that entices passersby. Inside, two floors are separated by the structural raw concrete, with ducts left exposed, and double-height windows provide plenty of light. The furniture, by Pin Stone Gallery, The Foundry and Yothaka, as well as photo and product design exhibitions, showcase the skills of local artisans. Upstairs is more business-like, with communal tables and a meeting room for hire. Keep the grey matter ticking over with healthy, global, homemade comfort dishes such as the quinoa salad with asparagus, green bean and zucchini. A selection of wines, beers and simple, refreshing cocktails makes Storyline a popular evening hangout too.
*Nusra Building, 3/3 Sukhumvit Soi 39,
T 062 941 5615*

URBAN LIFE

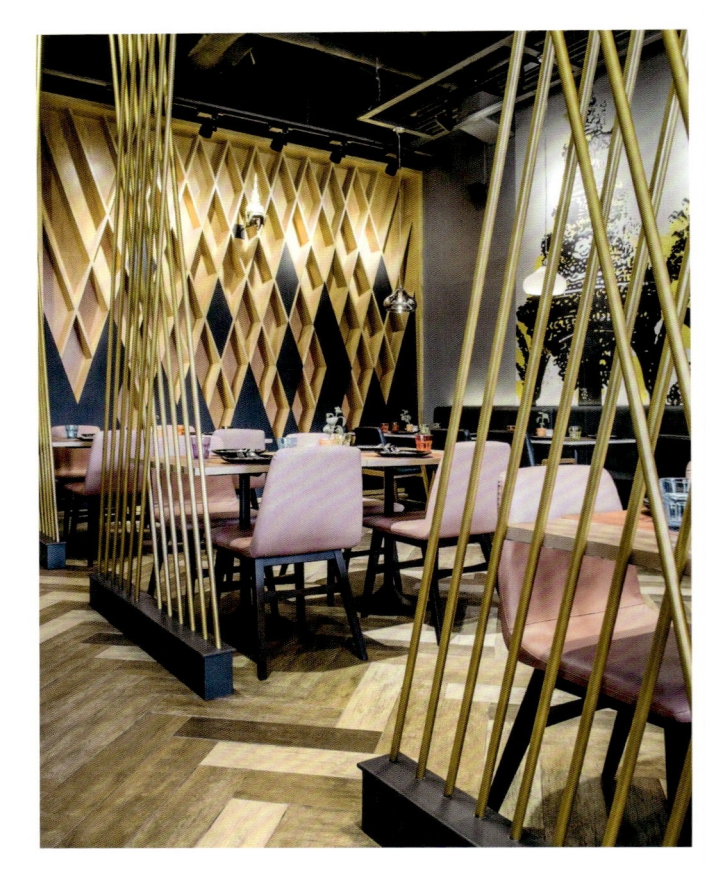

Osha

Unusually, this Thai restaurant is imported, having launched in San Francisco, where it won plaudits for melding contemporary techniques with the tenets of traditional cuisine. And it does not disappoint here either, evidenced by the well-heeled locals who pack it out every night. The moody neon-lit entrance looks as if it could lead to a high-end nightclub, and the flamboyant interior has a gold-on-purple theme, an enormous *chada* (crown) over the bar, a spiral staircase and upstairs walls painted with murals that depict scenes from the *Ramayana*. The menu provides a spin on the classics, exemplified by a rendition of *pad krapao* (a working man's staple of stir-fried meat with holy basil and chilli), made with Kagoshima Wagyu beef and confit egg. *99 Thanon Witthayu, T 02 256 6555, www.oshabangkok.com*

Teens of Thailand

Gin is the focus at this bijou venue, one of a burgeoning contingent of bars, galleries and dining spots in happening Talad Noi. Behind heavy wooden doors lies a minimal interior in which the characteristics and quirks of the 80-year-old shophouse are laid bare. Mismatched vintage furniture and wicker stools dot the concrete floor, mood lighting keeps things atmospheric, and photography and posters adorn the walls. Behind the tiny bar, a team led by Niks Anuman-Rajadhon raid an enormous contingent of potions to make classic and bespoke cocktails. The house G&T, mixed with local herbs and spices, is a speciality. The laidback ethos contrasts with the name of the place – a reference to the crazy kids who bomb around town on motorbikes.
76 Soi Nana, Thanon Rama IV,
T 081 443 3784

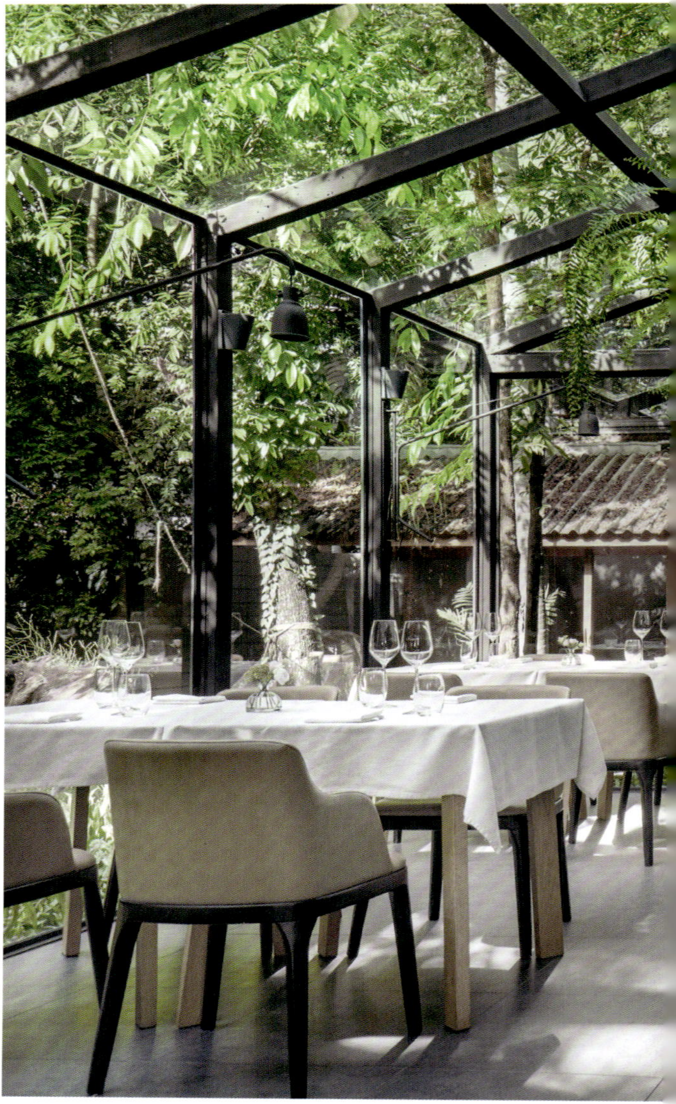

Sühring

Twin chefs Thomas and Mathias Sühring retained the soul of their gorgeous 1970s villa (Wintergarten, pictured) when they converted it into this delightful setting in which to serve modern German cuisine. The small plates concept takes in pickling and smoking, and cutting-edge methods, in dishes typified by the *Spätzle* (soft egg noodle) with roasted pork knuckle.
10 Soi Yenakat 3, T 02 287 1799

Café Now by Propaganda

Satit Kalawantavanich launched product design brand Propaganda in 1996 and its whimsical offerings struck a chord with the Thai sense of fun. The playful, plastic pieces are usually inspired by animals or anatomy, from stools shaped like molars to a shark's jaw bottle opener and a ballerina dustpan and brush. In 2015, the firm took a new direction, converting part of its office in Lat Phrao into the industrial-vintage Café Now (T 098 308 8210). A year later it opened this second branch, a white-tiled space partitioned by metal-mesh screens. Now you can browse its wares, and those from other Thai firms, like Rubber Killer's recycled bags, over a locally roasted coffee, ginger latte or mocktail such as the Zaap, a mix of tom yum, passionfruit and lemon.
3rd floor, Siam Discovery, Thanon Rama I, T 02 658 0430

Tep Bar

Hidden away down an alley off the action-packed Soi Nana, this authentic venue pays homage to the culture of central Thailand. Tep means 'deity' and drinks can appear to have divine qualities – it's no coincidence that rural hoedowns are boisterous affairs. Potent libations such as house-infused *ya dong* (herbal whisky) and *bangfai phayanak* (beer and herbal liquor), and surprising concoctions like *ya sanae* (rum with roselle and butterfly pea juice), are served up in glasses, wooden cups and ornate copper goblets. Snacks include *moo sarong* (pork balls fried in a yellow noodle wrap) and *khao kriab wow* (rice crackers with chilli paste). Live performances of classical, jazz and traditional music, which is often played on the xylophone, flute and barrel drum, start around 7.30pm (except Mondays).
69-71 Soi Nana, T 098 467 2944

Quince

In a charming 1950s house conversion, part furnished by neighbouring interiors store Casa Pagoda (T 02 258 1917), Quince serves an all-day Mediterranean menu to a well-heeled crowd. The buzzy front room has steel-framed glass walls that look out onto a garden patio, and the high ceilings and industrial elements lend it a loft-style chic. At the rear is a more intimate space (right) with whitewashed brickwork, wood floors, a walk-in wine cellar, retro items and a vintage chandelier. The kitchen is laudably particular about provenance and sources ingredients from Thai farms; dairy is from Hua Hin, lamb from Pakchong, and vegetables from the Royal Projects and city markets. Cocktails are crafted with house-made potions – the Ginger Collins is mixed with Iron Balls artisan gin, cold-pressed green ginger juice and aromatic bitters.
Sukhumvit Soi 45, T 02 662 4478, www.quincebangkok.com

URBAN LIFE

Bamboo Chic Bar
Although predominantly a slick, secluded retreat for a drink, Bamboo Chic also offers inventive snacks including skewers from the robata grill. However, the star of the show is its extensive selection of sakes, wines and signature cocktails, such as the Bamboo Crush, mixed with Chivas Regal, ginger ale and apple juice. Orbit Design Studio's interior concept features a couple of massive Egyptian chandeliers and an underlit walkway that ushers you through the dark entrance. Nearby, another hotel haunt worth a trip is 22 Kitchen & Bar at the Dusit Thani (see p087), which serves pan-Pacific cuisine, and has a panorama over Lumphini Park and the Royal Bangkok Sports Club, right up to Ratchaprasong.
4th floor, Le Méridien, 40/5 Thanon Surawong, T 02 232 8888, www.lemeridienbangkokpatpong.com

Bo.lan

Former students of David Thompson, the Michelin-starred chef at Nahm (see p066), Duangporn Songvisava (Bo) and Dylan Jones (lan) opened Bo.lan in 2009. The name is also a subtle play on the word *boran*, meaning 'ancient', and the menu would not be out of place in the courts of the Sukhothai and Ayutthaya periods. The fragrant, delicate taste of dishes such as *tom klong*, a hot soup with smoked fish, and stir-fried squid with palm heart and red chillies, expertly showcases the impressive breadth of Thai cooking. The interior is adorned with lampshades fashioned out of *gra dong* (traditional flat baskets made from bamboo used for drying chillies and fish) and a rotating selection of exquisite Thai artwork.
24 Sukhumvit Soi 53, T 02 260 2962, www.bolan.co.th

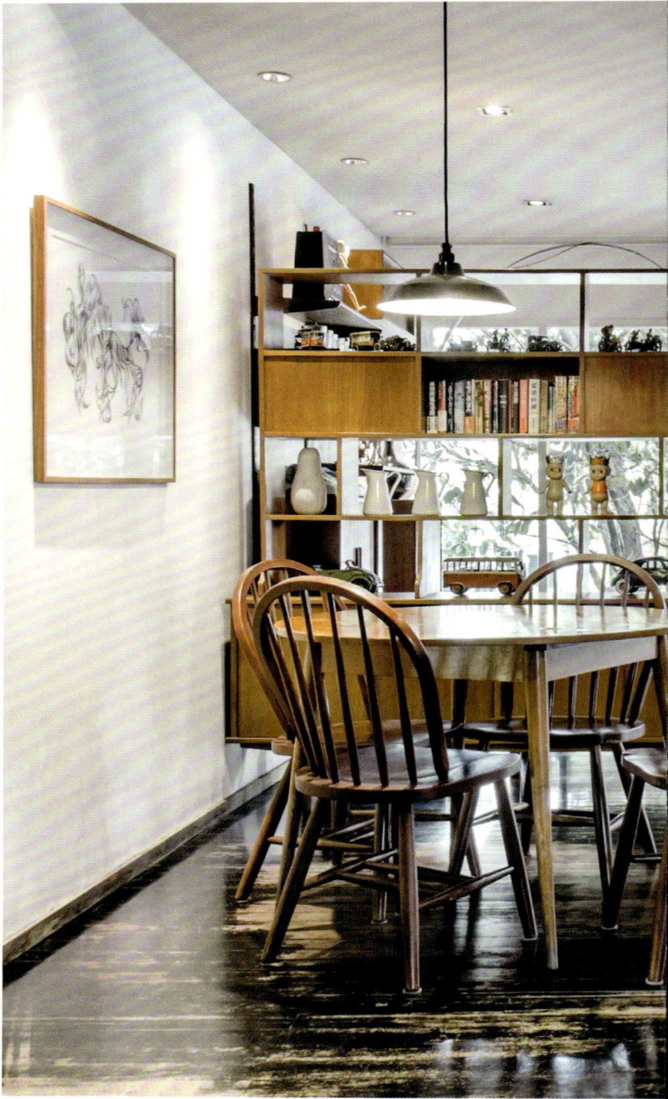

Vanilla Garden

The Ekkamai flagship of local restaurant group Vanilla encompasses three separate buildings surrounding a central fountain in an English-style garden. Vanilla Bakehouse proffers light meals as well as an array of pastries, breads and desserts – try the signature Ring, a cronut topped with ice cream, caramel and custard – and Vanilla Project, which has a double-height glass front, functions as the office. The visual star of the compound is the 1960s-style Vanilla Café, which is set in a low-rise two-storey house. Heavily laden bookshelves create partitions and the varnished wood floors and a collection of vintage toys and Japanese comics all add to the charm. The mix of mainly Japanese and Italian dishes can be rather hit and miss, but the pretty setting makes it worth the effort alone.
53 Ekkamai Soi 12, Sukhumvit Soi 63, T 02 381 6120, www.vanillaindustry.com

Salt

Leafy Ari is about as close as Bangkok gets to being bohemian and it bustles with boutiques, coffee shops and young arty types. Salt opened in 2011 and sits on a quiet corner of Soi 4. Designer Antika Teparak converted this concrete shell of a former sales office into a minimalist glass box, with floor-to-ceiling windows, marble tables and a terrace with a small rock garden. A lounge area was added in 2012, a wine cellar the year after, and a whisky room called Eleventwelfth in 2015. The cuisine is a mix of Japanese, Italian and French given a local twist – perhaps carpaccio with a Thai dressing, or rib-eye with wasabi sauce. From the cocktail list, try the Bangkok Mule, which is a blend of Mekhong rum, lemongrass and ginger ale.
111/2 Thanon Phahon Yothin 7 / Ari Soi 4, T 02 619 6886, www.saltbangkok.com

Sirocco

This extraordinary spot is perched 209m up on the 63rd floor of the State Tower (see p011). A skywalk stretches right out over the city and has a circular bar, which changes colour at night, and where you might well need a stiff drink to settle the nerves. The alfresco restaurant has a grand cinematic setting, due to its Romanesque columns under a golden dome, takes its name from the Mediterranean wind, and serves mains like Nova Scotia lobster and Wagyu short ribs, but is any of that really what you're here for? Other great rooftop hangouts include Octave (T 02 797 0000) at the Marriott Sukhumvit, and Vertigo and Moon Bar (T 02 679 1200) on the 61st floor of the Banyan Tree, which has a fine view of the MahaNakhon Tower (see p012). *Lebua at State Tower, 1055 Thanon Silom, T 02 624 9555, www.lebua.com*

Nahm

The original incarnation of Nahm in The Halkin hotel in London was the first Thai restaurant to win a Michelin star. In 2010, Aussie chef David Thompson opened this Bangkok outpost, causing much debate about whether a *farang* (Westerner) could cook authentic food. He proved doubters wrong. Many of Thompson's dishes, such as smoked fish curry with prawns; chicken livers and cockles; and stir-fried frogs' legs, are based on recipes from the royal court, and desserts are created by his long-time collaborator Tanongsak Yordwai. Japanese designer Koichiro Ikebuchi has installed layered red-brick columns, inspired by the temples of Ayutthaya, lattice screens, silk furnishings and tables made of teak. The venue overlooks a pretty outdoor pool.
Metropolitan by COMO, 27 Thanon Sathorn Tai, T 02 625 3333, www.comohotels.com

URBAN LIFE

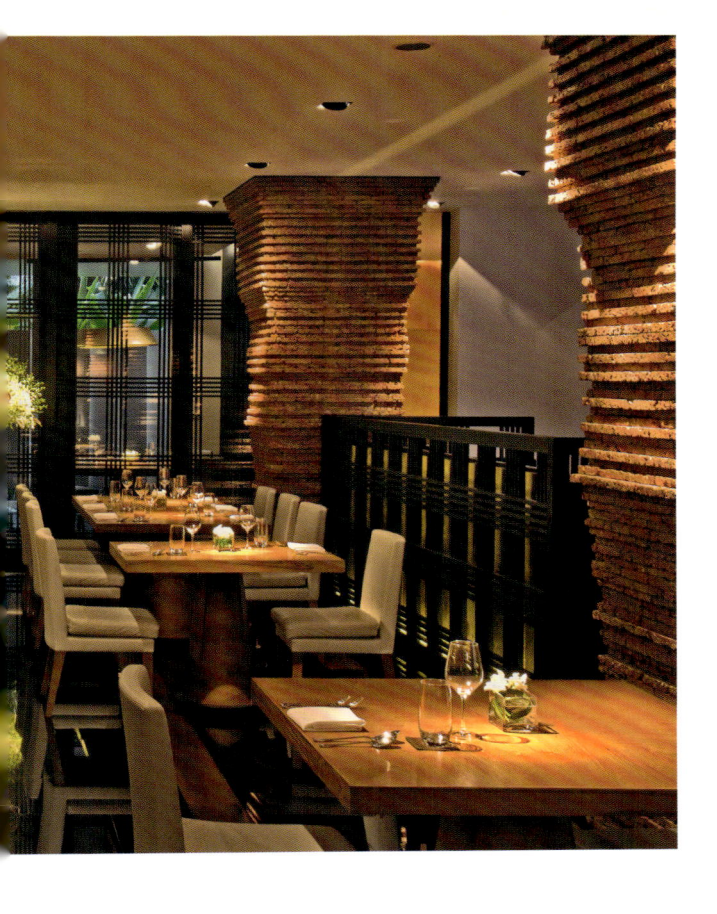

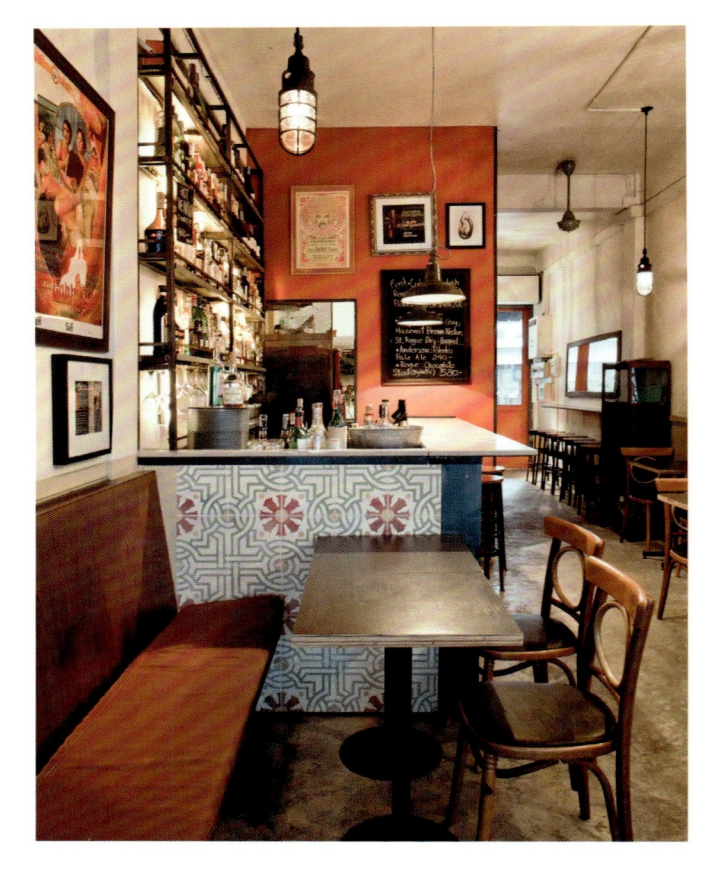

WTF Gallery & Café

One of the pioneers of the craft cocktail movement, WTF opened in 2010 and has teemed with creatives, journalists and the NGO crowd ever since, excited to see the likes of Sazerac on the drinks list. Vintage shophouse doors act as partitions, and the walls and wood panelling are decorated with retro Thai movie posters and historical ephemera from across Southeast Asia. An upstairs gallery showcases exhibitions by emerging, mainly local, artists, and there are occasional events, including poetry readings, story-tellings, intimate gigs and DJ sessions. Drop by to sample one of the excellent house cocktails, such as the Muay Thai Punch. There is no food, but you can order in from the Crying Thaiger (T 097 052 8861) meat shack over the road.
7 Sukhumvit Soi 51, T 02 662 6246, www.wtfbangkok.com

Soul Food Mahanakorn

For hearty local cuisine, pay a visit to Soul Food, a three-storey shophouse near the start of Thonglor. As the name suggests, the restaurant serves comfort dishes in a cosy setting. Highlights include *khao soi*, a mild northern curry with crunchy noodles; and *mieng kham*, lettuce leaves in which to wrap chilli, lime, peanuts and tamarind sauce. Rotating specials keep things fresh. Owner Jarrett Wrisley, a food writer turned restaurateur, designed the space and will squeeze you in upstairs if the ground floor (above) is full, which it often is. Works by global artists line the panelled walls and simple Scandinavian-style furniture sits on polished concrete. Both the potent cocktails and on-point soundtrack keep the expat crowd happy.
56/10 Sukhumvit Soi 55, T 02 714 7708, www.soulfoodmahanakorn.com

INSIDER'S GUIDE
AU EKBUTR UDOMPHOL, FASHION DESIGNER

Rising fashion star Au Ekbutr lives in the heart of the Sukhumvit action. 'Bangkok is a chaotic and delicious mess, the harmonious coexistence of high and low, old and new,' he says. To avoid traffic snarl-ups, he hops about on public transport, motorbike taxis and the ferries that ply the Chao Phraya, perhaps to the multi-brand boutique Siwilai (see p088) or to check out the latest shows at RMA Institute (see p034) and CityCity (see p076). He is also a big fan of The Jam Factory (see p040): 'A great set-up by the river, with an outdoor market, a restaurant, a gallery and occasional live bands.'

In the evenings, Ekbutr likes to dine at Bunker (see p046) or Err (394/35 Thanon Maharaj, T 02 622 2291), set in an old shophouse, where the menu is curated by Bo.lan (see p061): 'Casual but tasty Thai – try the crispy chicken skin.' Then he might head to Studio Lam (3/1 Sukhumvit Soi 51, T 02 261 6661), for its 'retro sounds and understated interiors', Dark Bar (2nd floor, Ekkamai Mall, Ekkamai Soi 10, T 092 446 6298), which has an 'intimate vibe', or, when an event is on, Future Factory (1077/48 Thanon Phahonyothin, T 098 253 9356): 'Obscure gigs, DJs and exhibitions.' If it has been a late one, he'll be tempted by the 'legendary grilled pork skewers' sold on Soi Convent. To get rid of the cobwebs the morning after, he suggests a bike tour to the jungle in Bang Krachao. Or for something more relaxing, he'll escape to the beach at Hua Hin (see p096).
For full addresses, see Resources.

URBAN LIFE

ART AND DESIGN
GALLERIES, STUDIOS AND PUBLIC SPACES

The modernisation of visual culture can be traced back to 1933 when Corrado Feroci founded the School of Fine Arts. The Italian sculptor adopted the name Silpa Bhirasri (see p038), designed the city's Democracy Monument, and inspired masters such as Thawan Duchanee and Chalermchai Kositpipat, whose work can be seen at MOCA (see p042). Yet for decades the scene struggled to overcome institutionalised ideals of aesthetics and religion in Thai art. This finally changed as the political climate mellowed in the late 1990s, the government invested in the arts, and society rapidly globalised. H Gallery (see p078) and 100 Tonson (see p079) pioneered the private sector and it has flourished ever since. There are two major hubs: Sathorn, home to glossy ventures like CityCity (see p076), and the Old Town, where rawer spaces often double as bars – see Soy Sauce Factory (11/1 Charoen Krung Soi 24, T 061 835 6824) and Cho Why (17 Soi Nan, Thanon Charoen Krung), and the more polished Serindia (Charoen Krung Soi 36, T 02 238 6410).

Meanwhile, Bangkok-based artisans, from Thinkk Studio (see p089) to P Tendercool (see p074), are harnessing craft techniques, traditional motifs and native materials into contemporary design. Sample this creative energy at Objects of Desire (see p088), where, alongside PDM's graphic rugs and R Noo's cement vases, you'll find conceptual items by Trimode (see p075) and 56th Studio (see p093).
For full addresses, see Resources.

YenakArt Villa

Set in a Bauhaus-flavoured new-build with double-height ceilings and an alabaster-hued interior, YenakArt Villa was launched in 2015 by Frenchman Jeremy Opritesco. Exhibitions rotate every six weeks, flipping between well-known artists whose work is connected to the region, and interesting young talent such as painter Padungpong Saruno. The 2016 show 'Back to the Moon' by the pre-eminent Thai sculptor Sivadol Sitipol featured pieces, some up to 5m high, made from stone, brass, bronze and marble, and mused on the state of society and the environment. Pop-up art dinner parties here are some of the most sought-after invites in town. It's open 3pm to 7pm Wednesday to Friday, and 11am to 7pm on Saturday; otherwise by appointment.
69 Soi Prasat Suk, Thanon Yen Akat,
T 02 671 9413, www.yenakartvilla.com

P Tendercool

In a growing creative enclave behind TCDC (see p038), P Tendercool specialises in beautiful bespoke tables made from slabs of antique exotic hardwood, and reclaimed wood from vintage houses and rice barns. There is a debt to Scandi minimalism and Shaker simplicity, but the materials, and techniques of local carpenters, keep them rooted in Thailand. The hand-cast bronze, aluminium and brass work is supervised by an Italian maestro who once worked with Salvador Dalí. Raw woods are racked up in a WWII riverside warehouse, and the furniture (the firm also makes chairs and sofas) is showcased in an art deco building alongside art and interior objects by other designers (light sculptures by Eric Poisson and paintings by Jean-Louis Dulaar, above).
48-58 Soi Thanon Charoen 30,
T 02 266 4344, www.ptendercool.com

Trimode Studio

The multidisciplinary trio behind Trimode Studio have created stylish interiors for a number of the city's hippest eateries. The firm also produces design items, including the 'Nine Elements' marble paperweight (above), created as a tribute to the late ninth monarch, and furniture, such as the 'Diamond', a glossy, faceted lounger, and 'Walk' chair, which appears to be on the move. Trimode Accessories is a neat line in jewellery, too. Elsewhere, Anon Pairot (T 02 381 6799) is leading the charge of this new generation of designers. His work often incorporates sustainable materials like cassava, the basis for his sculptural 'Penta' hanging lamps; and the 'Cell' easy chair and ottoman, which have a spider's web aesthetic, were produced using a low-waste method of aluminium casting.
T 081 849 9925, www.trimodestudio.com

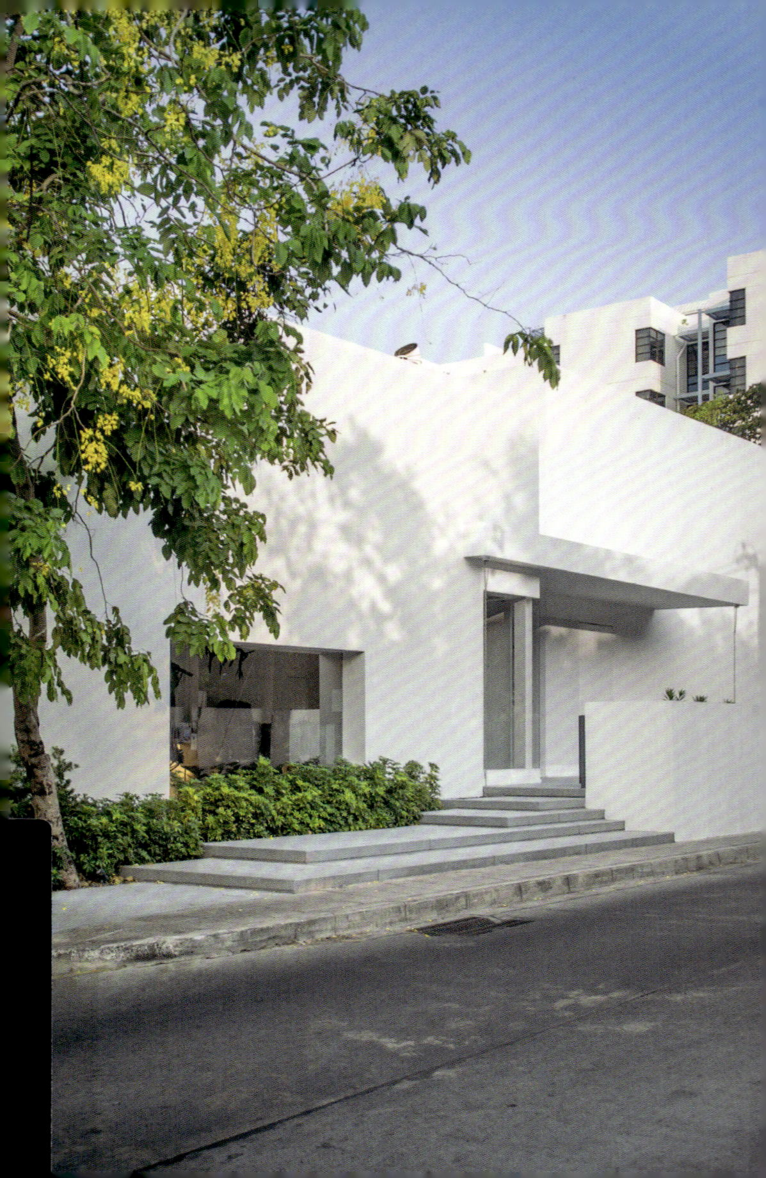

Bangkok CityCity Gallery

In the shadows of Sathorn's skyscrapers are some of Bangkok's slickest galleries, such as this purpose-built pair of cleverly integrated concrete boxes by architects Site-Specific. A cut-out window onto the street reveals a taster of what's inside the smaller room, skylights and openings at floor level brighten the main space, and a courtyard is used for video installations and live performances. Collectors Akapol Sudasna, who makes documentaries on youth culture, and Supamas Phahulo, a former curator at TCDC (see p038), focus on emerging Thai talent like cartoonist Wisut Ponnimit. 'Dream Property' (above), by Miti Ruangkritya, is an ongoing project about city real-estate speculation. Open Wednesdays to Saturdays, 1pm to 7pm.
13/3 Sathorn Soi 1, Thannon Sathorn Tai, T 083 087 2725, www.bangkokcitycity.com

H Gallery

US-born Ernst H Lee founded this gallery in a late 19th-century colonial mansion in 2002 to focus exclusively on Thai artists. The scope has broadened to encompass all of Southeast Asia, and since teaming up with Irishman Brian Curtin in 2011, it launched the upstairs H Space as a more experimental platform, juxtaposed with the warm wood tones and furnishings of this 125-year-old building. For instance, 'Scenes from the Life of Paris' (above) was a video installation by Gary Carsley that turned two busts by Italian sculptor Canova into ventriloquist's dummies in a play on time and meaning. There's plenty of local talent on the roster, not least textile artist Jakkai Siributr, and master of abstraction Somboon Hormtientong. Closed Tuesdays.
201 Sathorn Soi 12, T 085 021 5508, www.hgallerybkk.com

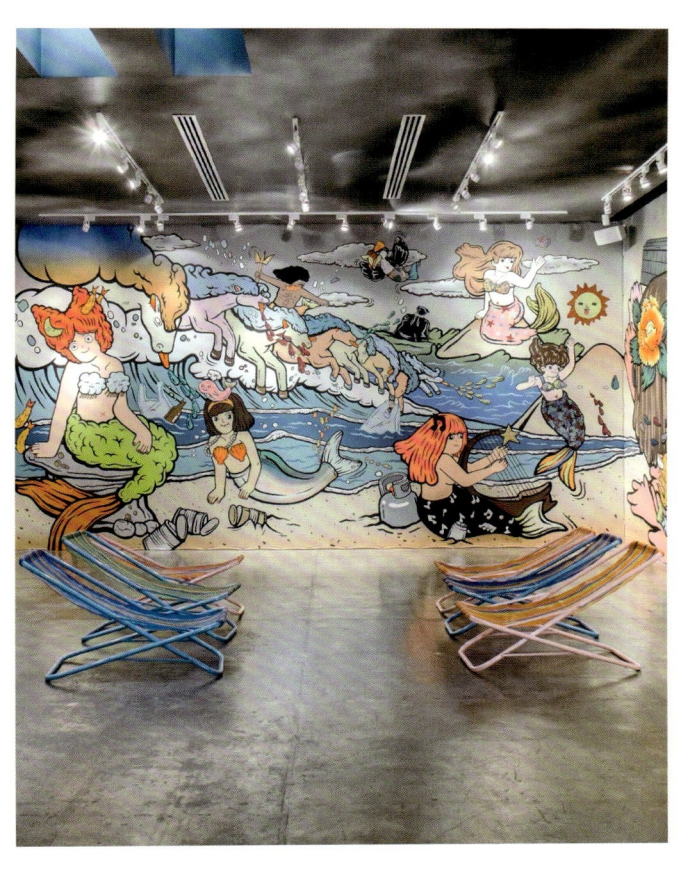

100 Tonson Gallery

The first gallery in the country to exhibit at Art Basel, in 2011, is still one of its heaviest hitters. Christian Liaigre was commissioned to convert a house in a swanky residential district into this elegant space in 2003. It has brought headline names to Bangkok, including Damien Hirst and Yayoi Kusama, but the overriding ethos is to promote Thai talent. Gallerist Ek-anong 'Aey' Phanachet puts on shows by prominent figures like Pinaree Sanpitak, who explores femininity in various media, and painter Phaptawan Suwannakudt, and continues to champion up-and-coming artists — Yuree Kensaku's site-specific mural 'Atmosfear' (above) was typical of her lively, colourful, stream-of-consciousness pieces, which mine popular culture. The creative set flock to openings.
100 Soi Tonson, Thanon Ploenchit,
T 02 010 5813, www.100tonsongallery.com

ARCHITOUR
A GUIDE TO BANGKOK'S ICONIC BUILDINGS

Of all the dirty, congested, unplanned metropolises in Asia, there is none more inspiring than Bangkok. If it was not for the manner in which its highways, municipal structures and 1960s bungalows all collide in a mad, buzzing pile, the city would not be where it is now – teetering on the verge of a new movement in design (and, one hopes, architecture). The modern city seems chaotic at first, but is well-patterned at a distance. The 18th- and 19th-century wooden homes and ancient palaces are remnants of the last fluid era with a purely Thai plan. Since then, Western and local ideas have fused, a trend that reached its peak with the Dusit Thani (see p087).

Monumental malls continue to sprout (see p013), yet the likes of the Face Bangkok complex (29 Sukhumvit Soi 38, T 02 713 6048) and Jam Factory (see p040) indicate a low-rise backlash. Of other recent interventions, the Skytrain excels for its transformation of urban space, and its great concrete arches and flyovers have added a *Blade Runner*-esque brutalism that seems entirely appropriate here. There have been few notable additions to the skyline, apart from Raimon Land's condo The River (Soi Charoen Nakhon 13) and the MahaNakhon (see p012), the showpiece the city so desperately craved. Yet even without a clutch of contemporary buildings to put it on the world map, Bangkok's tangled, singular landscape does at least force one to see things differently, and in a very Thai context.
For full addresses, see Resources.

Suvarnabhumi Airport

A new airport for Bangkok was proposed in the early 1970s, but politics and financing kept plans on the ground until 2002, when construction began. Four years later, its two runways finally alleviated the almighty crush at Don Mueang. Two further phases of expansion will enable Suvarnabhumi to handle 90 million travellers a year by 2021. Designed by architects Jahn, its abstracted H-shaped plan comprises a central hub, off which lead glass tubes shaded by trellises of translucent fabric and flanked by some impressive landscaping. Those who have complained of long treks to gates perhaps did not look up to see the world's tallest freestanding control tower, at 132m, even if its slender form is more factory chimney than the usual UFO-on-a-stick. The people-watching as 'couples' say goodbye remains as entertaining (and excruciating) as ever.

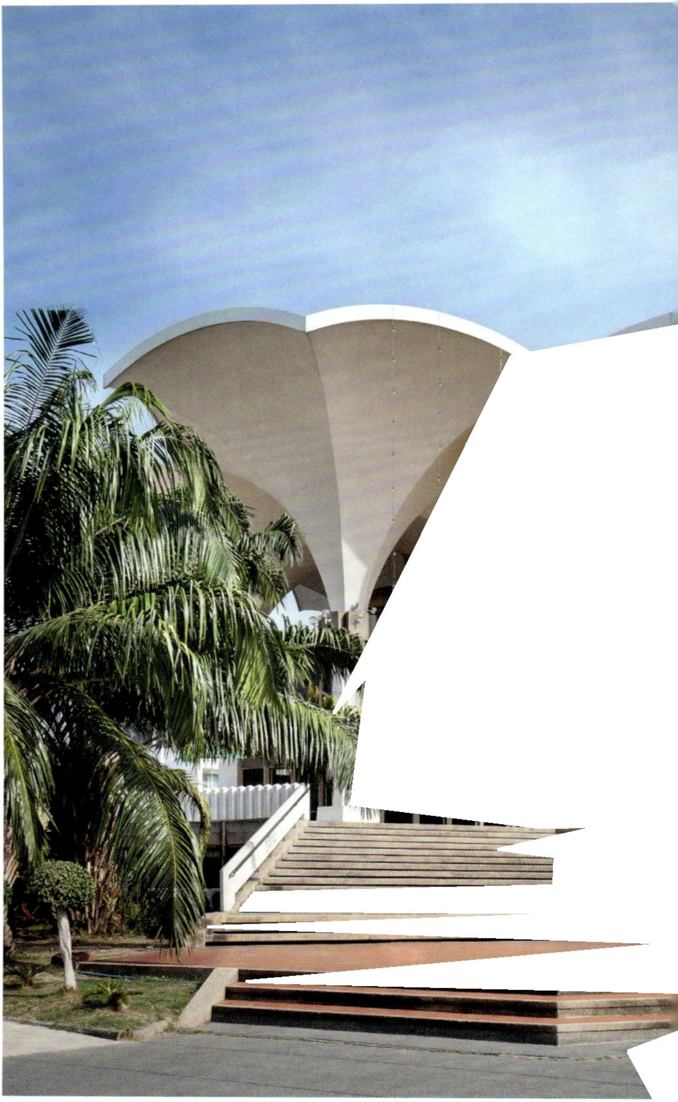

Islamic Centre of Thailand
Bangkok's largest mosque is a triumph of organic shapes and Moorish and Arabian motifs by architect Paichit Pongpanluk that was unveiled in 1971. Saddled with a limited budget, he devised a modular, hexagonal system of 19 sculpted-concrete 'flowers', each one featuring six 'petals' and with a diameter of 12m. Supported on slender columns, they evoke lilies in bloom and connect to form a roof canopy, while the 'stems' conceal pipes to drain rainwater. Incorporated into this overall scheme, two prayer halls accommodate up to 5,000 worshippers. The soaring ceilings and curvature of the design aid natural ventilation to compensate for the lack of air-conditioning. Inside, small windows of pink stained glass add a jolt of colour above the 21 black marble slabs that are carved with verses from the Koran and indicate the direction of Mecca.
87/2 Thanon Ramkhamhaeng, Soi 2

Siri Apartment Building

Architect Dan Wongprasat took the circle to its zenith in 1970 in this soft-brutalist apartment block that's often compared to a spaceship or an octopus. Yet its design is as functional as its looks are eccentric. The floorplan encases a void that maximises ventilation and provides natural light. It is supported on 12 cylinders with porthole windows that house the bathrooms and kitchens, with lounges and bedrooms set back behind balconies to limit exposure to the sun. Wongprasat followed up the theme at the 1974 Ambassador Sukhumvit (171 Sukhumvit Soi 11) and then the 1990 Holiday Inn Silom (981 Thanon Silom), two of the city's iconic older hotels, but neither is as eminently practical as Siri, where his concept was executed beautifully and, as a result, units are still highly sought-after.
59 Thanon Witthayu

Robot Building

At ground level, there is not a great deal to distinguish the Bangkok headquarters of the United Overseas Bank (UOB) from any other high-rise lining the gridlocked Thanon Sathorn. However, when viewed from afar (the Skytrain between Surasak and Chong Nonsi stations, say), architect Sumet Jumsai's 83m-high design jumps out. Tagged the 'Robot', it was inspired by one of his son's toys and was completed in 1986. The staggered shape rises through 20 floors, its 6m-diameter 'eyeballs' of reflective glass forming windows, hooded by metal-louvred 'eyelids'. The rooftop communication antennae double up as lightning rods and the 'caterpillar wheels' and reinforced concrete 'nuts' adorning the building also have a practical function as unusual window casings and sunshades.
191 Thanon Sathorn Tai

The Met

Singapore architects WOHA designed this 2009 prototype for high-density living in the tropics by brilliantly extrapolating the low-rise model into a naturally ventilated, eco-friendly, 228m-high tower. The 370 north-south-facing condo units occupy three separate blocks connected every five storeys by sky terraces, both public and private, allowing breezes to penetrate deep within. All the horizontal surfaces are planted with vegetation, creepers act as sun screens, and individual recessed terraces further reduce the heat levels. Cleverly grounding The Met in its setting, the cladding resembles Thai ceramic tiles, staggered balconies are reminiscent of those seen in traditional timber houses, and walls inlaid with stainless-steel panels reference the mirrors in local temples.
123 Thanon Sathorn Tai

Dusit Thani

The tallest building in the city for at least a few months after its opening in 1970, this hotel is a rare project, reflecting art deco and modernist influences in a manner that's clearly Thai. Note, too, the influence of Buddhist architecture in the portico-like frames and overall shape. Arresting at night, when the geometrical, gold-lined elements that run up the facade are lit, it's symbolic to Bangkok residents because it is locally owned and was one of the first structures in the city to make a high-rise statement. For expats, the way in which the Dusit Thani has successfully melded Eastern elements in a Western context makes for a point of conversation – one which should ideally be held over a few cocktails in the top-floor bar (see p060).
946 Thanon Rama IV, T 02 200 9000, www.dusit.com

SHOPS
THE BEST RETAIL THERAPY AND WHAT TO BUY

The fake Fendi and low-cost Lacoste that once blighted Bangkok's markets seem to finally be on the wane. Successive administrations have sought to promote the city as a fashion hub, and there has also been heavy investment in film, graphic design and other creative industries. The trailblazers include Pim Sukhahuta of Sretsis (2nd floor, Central Embassy, 1031 Thanon Phloenchit, T 02 160 5874), for whimsical womenswear, and Disaya Sorakraikitikul (see p094).

Destinations all unto themselves are Siwilai (5th floor, Central Embassy, 1031 Thanon Phloenchit, T 02 160 5809), a concept store with native labels (Victeerut, Vatanika), hip global brands (Sacai, Kitsune, Common Projects) and a café, and the outrageous vintage mash-up It's Happened To Be A Closet (124/1 Sukhumvit Soi 23, T 081 565 2026). Crafts to seek out include jewellery, such as the refined pieces at Atta (see p092), and ceramics – visit Yarnnakarn (2 Thanon Kamphaeng Phet, T 099 152 4635) for its hand-crafted vessels with an Astier de Villatte feel. Find lifestyle items, from totes to tapestries, at 2/7: Twice a Week (208 Soi Chula 50, T 087 507 1997). For an overview of the design scene, Objects of Desire (3rd floor, Siam Discovery, Thanon Rama I, T 02 685 1000) showcases 130 Thai makers, from local firm Cordesign Studio's wireless 'Klank' speakers covered in silk, to buffalo-horn bracelets and eco-friendly products like carpets made from krajood grass and water hyacinth. *For full addresses, see Resources.*

Thinkk Studio

After studying in northern Europe, Decha Archjananun and Ploypan Theerachai came back intent on integrating an understated aesthetic into local craftsmanship. Pieces such as the minimal 'Lines' shower bench, two interlocked pieces of polished teak, and the 'Epoch' ceramic collection, which melds ancient and modern methods, have a timeless feel. The 'Weight Vase' (above), THB7,500, deconstructs function into two clearly defined parts – a concrete base receptacle and a slender steel frame that plays with perception. Thinkk Studio has an outlet, Thingg, in Siam Discovery mall, which reopened in 2016 after a super-slick makeover into a 'lifestyle laboratory' by Nendo. On the same floor are Objects of Desire (opposite) and Café Now (see p056). *3rd floor, Siam Discovery, T 02 658 1000, www.thinkkstudio.com*

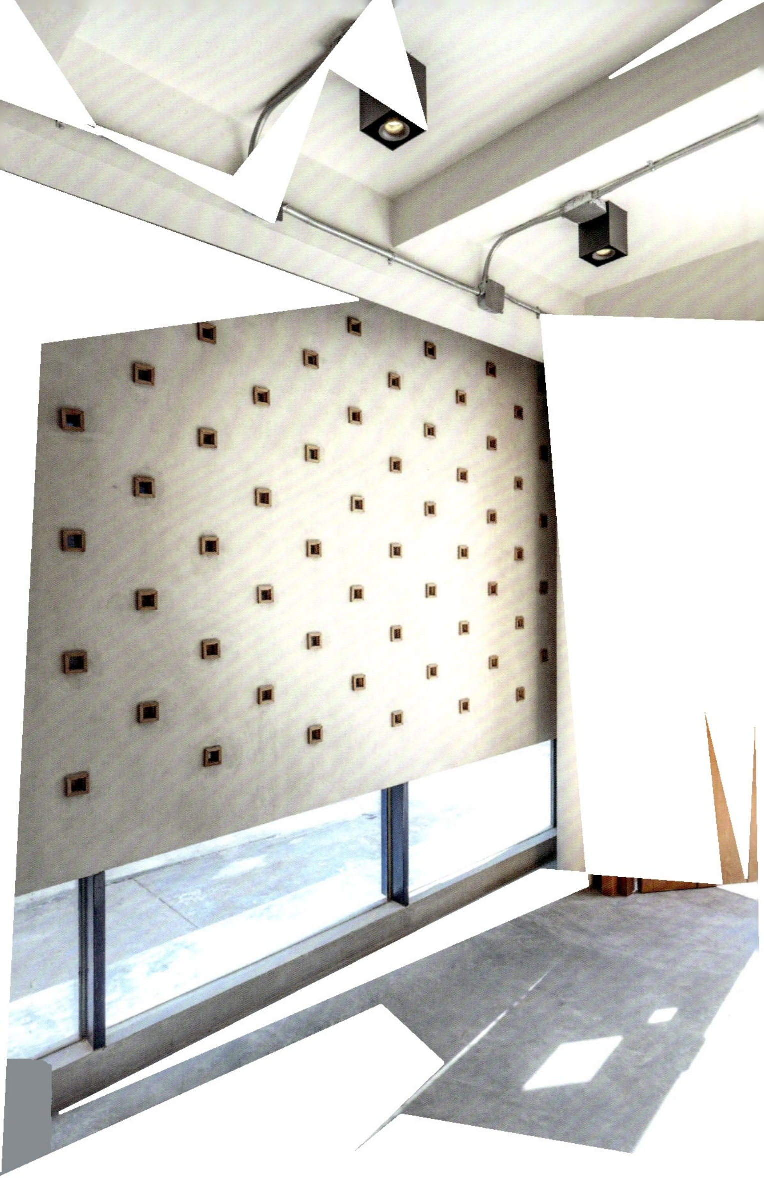

Keaton

There are plenty of tailors in Bangkok, but few are as unique as this one in Thonglor. It eschews the old-school persona of most gents' outfitters and the staff who implore potential clients to 'just take a look, sir'. In homage to the trade, PHTAA's neat concept evokes pattern cutting and peg plans, using a concrete and blue metal grid facade that is pierced with square holes. The design is repeated inside on the teak plywood desk and, together with the exposed brick, helps create a refined aesthetic. Owners Tatsura I-washita and Nantana Punbunjertkul use only top-quality fabrics in Keaton's ready-to-wear suits, shirts and trousers, as well as the bespoke service, which takes around a fortnight. Accessories include cufflinks, pocket squares and London Brown shoes.
77 Soi Chaemchan, Thonglor Soi 20,
T 097 042 4265

Atta Gallery

Occupying a pared-back but still stylishly funky space near the Chao Phraya, Atta offers statement hand-crafted jewellery by local and international makers. Look out for Thai designers, including Nutre Arayavanish, best known for her flat-pack pieces, which are made by connecting two-dimensional elements together to create 3D forms, and Munich-based Jiro Kamata, whose work incorporates iridescent mirror discs. The interiors feature walls hung with sculptural necklaces, while small stools, wooden screens and bulky concrete tables provide artful clutter. Fancy making your own? Enrol in a workshop at Smitheries, a hip jewellery studio/shop (T 086 336 5337) run by young talents Chaiwat Wattananukit and Piyamas Muenprasartdee.
4/6 Charoen Krung Soi 36, T 02 238 6422, www.attagallery.com

56th Studio

Charismatic duo Napawan and Saran Yen Panya draw inspiration from pop culture, and their hyper-fresh gallery/atelier/store showcases a flair for the offbeat and the kitsch, from custom-made furniture to graphic prints in big, brash motifs and eye-splitting bursts of colour. Projects have included the plastic 'Cheap Ass Elite' chair (above), a hybrid of a laundry basket and decorative legs that juxtaposes signifiers of high and low society, and a range of traditional Thai kitchen utensils given a makeover, like a Memphis-style coconut grater in black lacquer and gold leaf. You might also find pretty woven raffia bags festooned with pom poms by Wonder Cape Town and lighting by Thinkk Studio (see p091). Arty parties are a regular thing.
235/10 Sukhumvit Soi 31, T 02 662 1593, www.56thstudio.com

Disaya

Central Saint Martins graduate Disaya Sorakraikitikul debuted her womenswear brand internationally in 2007. Its ethos is romantic and flirty, often featuring bold colours, patterns and prints, tinged with a certain London attitude and eccentricity. Her signature cocktail dresses are notable for their flattering silhouettes, high-quality fabrics including velvet, satin and lace, and the details that add a contemporary twist, such as waist cut-outs, contrast seams and leather piecing. Her CentralWorld flagship (above) was designed by none other than Duangrit Bunnag (see p040), who installed lightwood floors, luminous perspex display cubes, and silver and rose-gold elements. There are now four (and counting) Disaya outlets in the city, in all the major malls.
2nd floor, Groove at CentralWorld, T 02 646 1828, www.disaya.com

Harnn

When it comes to Thai-style wellbeing, it's hard to beat a traditional massage, but the land of lemongrass has much more to offer the body. We picked up this organic Water Lily Facial Massage Oil (above), THB1,450 for 58g, by Harnn, a local brand that's stocked in 15 countries. Botanical ingredients, like vitamin E-rich extracts of rice-bran oil (an antioxidant with both anti-ageing and moisturising properties) are at the core of Harnn's range of natural hair, body and skincare products for men and women. The Bangkok flagship opened in 2005, with an interior design inspired by classic herbal medicine shops, a theme since repeated in all its branches. There are two outlets in CentralWorld as well as a standalone spa on the 12th floor.
3rd floor, CentralWorld, 999/9 Thanon Rama I, T 02 613 1429, www.harnn.com

ESCAPES

WHERE TO GO IF YOU WANT TO LEAVE TOWN

Paying due respect to the Thai love of extremes, if one leaves the sprawl and traffic of the city, it should really be for some kind of peace and an immersion in nature. You could drive the 90 minutes north to the UNESCO World Heritage temples of Ayutthaya, or head out west, where the seven-level waterfalls of Erawan, idyllic river scenery and the legendary bridge over the Kwai lure coachloads to Kanchanaburi. However, in our opinion, the best option is to do as most locals would when given the chance – go to the beach.

It is not always necessary to go all the way down to Koh Samui (opposite), Phuket or Koh Chang to find exotic scenery. Bangkok is, after all, a port, and the placid Gulf of Thailand is an hour's drive away. Take a trip to Koh Samet, a beautiful island and national park located approximately 200km south-east of the city, which is, by turns, a party paradise, a quiet respite or a family gathering place, depending on the chosen beach. For convenience and style, the best destinations are Hua Hin, thanks to the Anantara Resort & Spa (43/1 Thanon Phetkasem Beach, T 03 252 0250), and Kui Buri (see p102). The former was originally a fishing hamlet, but entered the spotlight when King Rama VII built a summer palace there. It has since become the Hamptons of Thailand, attracting a glitzy crowd, especially at weekends, due to its great hotels and seafood eateries, as well as an annual jazz festival and elephant polo tournament. *For full addresses, see Resources.*

The Library, Koh Samui

An hour's flight away, Thailand's second largest island is replete with monolithic Buddhas, palm-tree-fringed beaches and rainforested mountains. On the north-east coast, The Library, somewhat bizarrely, is a literary-inspired resort, but it avoids gimmickry due to a bold design aesthetic in which minimalist furniture and regional artworks play off a red, white and black palette. Even the library/bookshop itself, which is stocked with coffee-table pleasers, is housed in a glass-fronted pavilion by a striking crimson-hued pool. Further south, The Beach Samui (T 07 723 4567) opened in 2017, designed by Archer Humphryes and furnished by Yoo Studio. Its 21 suites have views over an archipelago that teems with life and is spectacular for snorkelling.
14/1 Moo 2, Chaweng Beach, Bo Phut, T 07 742 2767, www.thelibrarysamui.com

MAIIAM, Chiang Mai
This is perhaps Thailand's most cutting-edge art museum, as it fixes the spotlight firmly on native contemporary talent. It was designed by Bangkok firm All(zone), who converted a 3,000 sq m warehouse in an historic crafts district half an hour outside Chiang Mai. The facade is clad in thousands of mirror tiles that play with the light, a trick inspired by Thai temples. It displays the collection of Jean Michel Beurdeley, his late wife Patsri Bunnag and son Eric Bunnag Booth, which they have built up over the last 30 years. Look out for seminal works by Montien Boonma, Navin Rawanchaikul and Chatchai Puipia, while the inaugural show in 2016 was a retrospective of Chiang Mai filmmaker and artist Apichatpong Weerasethakul.
122 Moo 7, Tonpao, San Kamphaeng, www.maiiam.com

ESCAPES

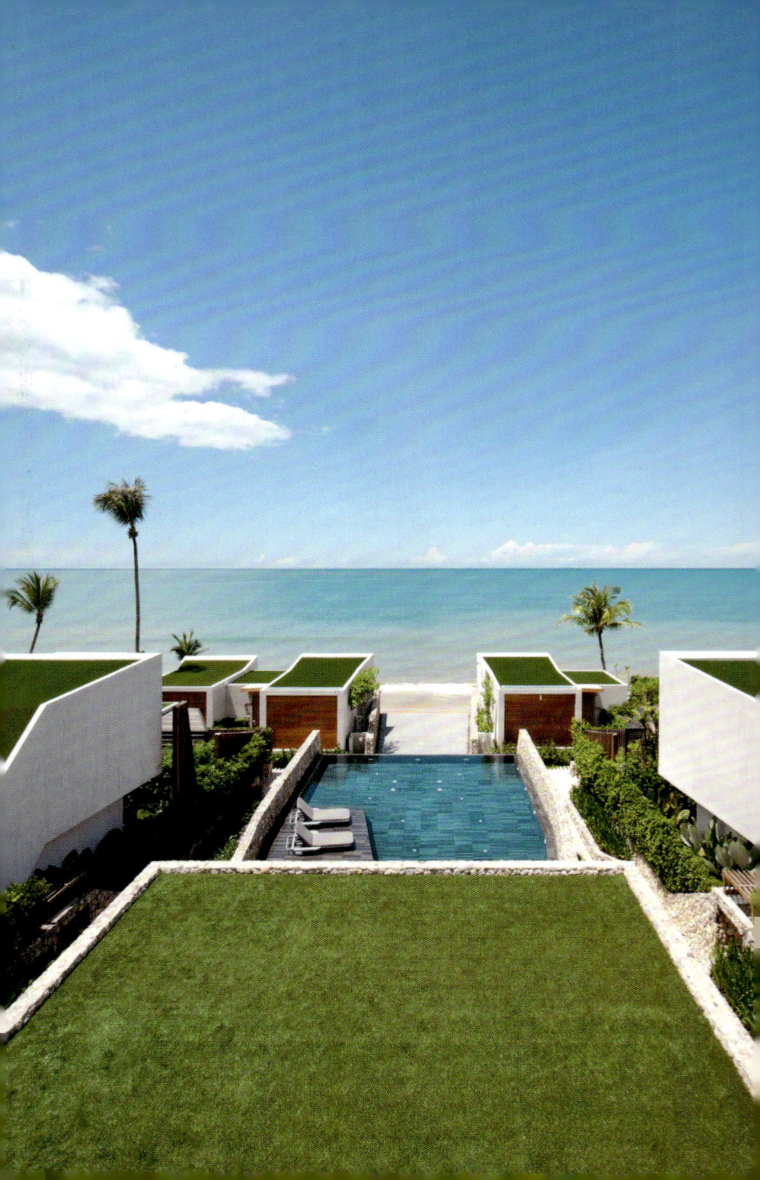

Casa de la Flora, Phang Nga

Facing the Andaman Sea, 90 minutes' drive from Phuket, these 36 modernist concrete-box villas were designed by VaSLab (see p017) and feature stone walls, grass roofs, cloistered wood decks, private pools and floor-to-ceiling windows. Interiors in all the rooms, as in the Casa Presidential Suite (above), are done out in teak, with custom-made furniture by Anon Pairot (see p075). An hour's drive further south, on Natai Beach, 11 high-profile designers, including the Campana brothers and Jaime Hayon, worked on the three villas and penthouse at the singular Iniala Beach House (T 07 645 1456). Other extravagances include a cinema, a Thai boxing ring, a games room with a Swarovski-studded pool table and a restaurant overseen by chef Tim Butler.
67/213 Moo 5, Khuk Khak, Khao Lak, T 07 642 8999, www.casadelaflora.com

X2 Kui Buri

Over the last decade, the cluster of villages situated around the once sleepy town of Hua Hin, 270km south of Bangkok, have seen an influx of jet-setters. A number of cutting-edge resorts have now opened in the surrounding area, at beaches such as Pranburi and in the pristine town of Kui Buri, a three-hour drive from the capital. This is the setting for the original outpost of X2, the design-led Thai resort company run by Bespoke Hospitality Management Asia. Twenty-three stylish villas stretch across a large site, each featuring bare rock and a glass front wall. Most of the accommodations have private pools, and four are on the beachfront, including the Luxury Pool Villa (above). A restaurant and bar offer sophisticated sustenance.
52 Moo 13, Aoi Noi, Muang, Prachuap Khiri Khan, T 03 251 0466, www.x2lobby.com

Six Senses Yao Noi

Sidestep Phuket, where cheap flights from all over Asia have led to mass-market hell, for one of the nearby islands. Ko Yao Noi is still relatively undiscovered, with pristine beaches, turquoise lagoons and limestone cliffs rising out of the sea, plus rice paddies and buffalo inland — Thai islands do not come much more Thai island than this. On the east coast, the Six Senses comprises 56 villas designed by Bangkok architects Habita, from one-bedroom hillside pads to four-bedroom mansions, each sequestered in the woods, with a pool and butler. Go rock-climbing or scuba-diving, or simply spend your days exploring the topography, either by kayak, yacht or helicopter. From Phuket, transfer here is by speedboat.
56 Moo 5, Tambol Koh Yao Noi, Amphur Koh Yao, Phang Nga, T 07 641 8500, www.sixsenses.com

NOTES
SKETCHES AND MEMOS

RESOURCES
CITY GUIDE DIRECTORY

A

Almeta 036
20/3 Sukhumvit Soi 23
T 02 258 4227
www.almeta.com

Ambassador Sukhumvit 084
171 Sukhumvit Soi 11

Anon Pairot 075
1/6 Ekkamai Soi 2
Thanon Sukhumvit 63
T 02 381 6799
www.anonpairot.com

Atta Gallery 092
4/6 Charoen Krung Soi 36
T 02 238 6422
www.attagallery.com

B

Baiyoke Tower II 009
222 Soi Ratchaprarop 3

Bamboo Chic Bar 060
4th floor
Le Méridien
40/5 Thanon Surawong
T 02 232 8888
www.lemeridienbangkokpatpong.com

Bangkok Art and Culture Centre 037
939 Thanon Rama I
T 02 214 6630
www.bacc.or.th

Bangkok CityCity Gallery 076
13/3 Sathorn Soi 1
Thanon Sathorn Tai
T 083 087 2725
www.bangkokcitycity.com

Beam 048
1st floor
72 Sukhumvit Soi 55
T 02 392 7750
www.beamclub.com

Bo.lan 061
24 Soi Sukhumvit 53
T 02 260 2962
www.bolan.co.th

Bunker 046
118/2 Sathorn Soi 12
T 092 563 9991
www.bunkerbkk.com

C

Café Now 056
Town In Town Soi 11
Lat Phrao
T 098 308 0430

Café Now by Propoganda 056
3rd floor
Siam Discovery
Thanon Rama I
T 02 658 0430

Casa Pagoda 058
45 Thanon Sukhumvit
T 02 258 1917
www.casapagoda.com

CAT Building 010
72 Thanon Charoen Krung
T 02 104 2372

Central Embassy 013
1031 Thanon Ploenchit
T 02 119 7777
www.centralembassy.com

Cho Why 072
17 Soi Nan
Thanon Charoen Krung

Crying Thaiger 068
27/1 Sukhumvit Soi 51
T 097 052 8861
www.thaigerbkk.com

D

Dark Bar 070
*2nd floor
Ekkamai Mall
Ekkamai Soi 10
T 092 446 6298
Open Wednesdays to Saturdays*
Democracy Monument 072
Thanon Ratchadamnoen Klang
Disaya 094
*2nd floor
Groove at CentralWorld
Thanon Ratchadamri
T 02 646 1828
www.disaya.com*
Dusit Thani 087
*946 Thanon Rama IV
T 02 200 9000
www.dusit.com*

E

Ekkamai Congee 033
*Ekkamai Soi 19
T 086 705 1251*
Elephant Tower 014
369/38 Thanon Phahon Yothin 26
Erawan Tea Room 044
*Grand Hyatt
494 Thanon Ploenchit
T 02 250 7777
www.erawanbangkok.com*
Err 070
*394/35 Thanon Maharaj
T 02 622 2291
www.errbkk.com*

F

56th Studio 093
*235/10 Sukhumvit Soi 31
T 02 662 1593
www.56thstudio.com*
Face Bangkok 080
*29 Sukhumvit Soi 38
T 02 713 6048*
Future Factory 070
*1077/48 Thanon Phahonyothin
T 098 253 9356
www.futurefactoryhq.com*

G

Gastro 1/6 034
*RMA Institute
238 Sukhumvit Soi 22
Soi Sai Nampthip 2
T 080 603 6421*
Grand Postal Building 038
*1160 Thanon Charoen Krung
T 02 105 7400*

H

H Gallery 078
*201 Sathorn Soi 12
T 085 021 5508
www.hgallerybkk.com*
Harnn 095
*3rd floor
CentralWorld
991/1 Thanon Rama I
T 02 613 1429
www.harnn.com*
Holiday Inn Silom 084
981 Thanon Silom

I

Ink & Lion Café 033
*1/7 Ekkamai Soi 2
Sukhumvit Soi 63
T 091 559 0994*

Islamic Centre of Thailand 082
87/2 Soi Thanon Ramkhamhaeng 2
Suan Luang
T 02 314 5638
www.thaiislamiccenter.com
It's Happened To Be A Closet 088
124/1 Sukhumvit Soi 23
T 081 565 2026

J
Jim Thompson House 036
6 Soi Kasemsan 2
Thanon Rama I
T 02 216 7368
www.jimthompsonhouse.com

K
Keaton 090
77 Soi Chaemchan
Thonglor Soi 20
T 097 042 4265

M
Magnolias Waterfront Residences 012
215 Thanon Charoen Nakorn
MahaNakhon Building 012
114 Thanon Narathiwat
T 02 234 1414
MAIIAM 098
122 Moo 7
Tonpao
San Kamphaeng
Chiang Mai
www.maiiam.com
The Met 086
123 Thanon Sathorn Tai
T 02 166 0000
www.met-bangkok.com

Museum of Contemporary Art 042
499 Thanon Kamphaengphet 6
Ladyao
T 02 016 5666
www.mocabangkok.com

N
Nahm 066
Metropolitan by COMO
27 Thanon Sathorn Tai
T 02 625 3333
www.comohotels.com
The Never Ending Summer 040
The Jam Factory
41/5 Thanon Charoen Nakhon
Khlong San
T 02 861 0953

O
100 Tonson Gallery 079
100 Soi Thanon
Thanon Ploenchit
T 02 010 5813
www.100tonsongallery.com
Objects of Desire 088
3rd floor
Siam Discovery
Thanon Rama I
T 02 685 1000
Octave 065
Marriott Sukhumvit
Sukhumvit Soi 57
T 02 797 0000
www.marriot.com
Osha 052
99 Thanon Witthayu
T 02 256 6555
www.oshabangkok.com

P
P Tendercool 074
48-58 Soi Thanon Charoen 30
T 02 266 4344
www.ptendercool.com
Pla Dib 048
1/1 Ari Soi Sampan 7
T 02 279 8185
www.pladibrestaurant.com

Q
Quince 058
Sukhumvit Soi 45
T 02 662 4478
www.quincebangkok.com

R
Rabbit Hole 048
125 Sukhumvit Soi 55
T 098 969 1335
The River 080
Soi Charoen Nakorn 13
www.theriverbangkok.com
RMA Institute 034
238 Sukhumvit Soi 22
Soi Sai Nampthip 2
T 02 663 0809
www.rmainstitute.net
Robot Building 085
191 Thanon Sathorn Tai
Royal Grand Palace 009
Thanon Na Phra Lan
Ruen-Nuad 032
42 Thanon Convent
T 02 632 2662

S
Salt 064
111/2 Thanon Phahon Yothin 7 / Ari Soi 4
T 02 619 6886
www.saltbangkok.com

Serindia 072
Op Garden
Charoen Krung Soi 36
T 02 238 6410
www.serindiagallery.com
Shugaa Dessert Bar 049
27 Sukhumvit Soi 61
T 02 381 5940
Siri Apartment Building 084
59 Thanon Witthayu
T 02 627 3955
Sirocco 065
Lebua at State Tower
1055 Thanon Silom
T 02 624 9999
www.lebua.com
Siwilai 088
5th floor
Central Embassy
1031 Thanon Ploenchit
T 02 160 5809
www.siwilaibkk.com
Smalls 048
186/3 Soi Suan Phlu 1
T 095 585 1398
Smitheries 092
2nd floor
Black Amber Building
Sukhumvit Soi 55
Thonglor Soi 5-7
T 086 336 5337
Soul Food Mahanakhorn 069
56/10 Sukhumvit Soi 55
T 02 714 7708
www.soulfoodmahanakorn.com
Soulbar 048
954 Thanon Charoen Krung
T 093 220 0441

Soy Sauce Factory 072
11/1 Charoen Krung Soi 24
T 061 835 6824
Sretsis 088
2nd floor
Central Embassy
1031 Thanon Ploenchit
T 02 160 5874
www.sretsis.com
State Tower 009
1055 Thanon Silom
Storyline 050
Nusra Building
3/3 Sukhumvit Soi 39
T 062 941 5615
Studio Lam 070
3/1 Sukhumvit Soi 51
T 02 261 6661
Sühring 054
10 Soi Yenakat 3
T 02 287 1799
www.suhringtwins.com
Suvarnabhumi Airport 081
999 Moo 1 Bangna
Thanon Trad
T 02 132 1888
www.suvarnabhumiairport.com

T
2/7: Twice a Week 088
208 Soi Chula 50
T 087 507 1997
22 Kitchen & Bar 060
Dusit Thani
946 Thanon Rama IV
T 02 200 9000
www.dusit.com

TCDC 038
Grand Postal Building
1160 Thanon Charoen Krung
T 02 105 7400
www.tcdc.or.th
Teens of Thailand 053
76 Soi Nana
Thanon Rama IV
T 081 443 3784
Tep Bar 057
69-71 Soi Nana
T 098 467 2944
Theera 033
Sukhumvit Soi 42
T 090 506 2222
Thinkk Studio 089
3rd floor
Siam Discovery
Thanon Rama I
T 02 658 1000
www.thinkkstudio.com
Trimode Studio 075
136/4 Newroad 82
Bangkoleam
T 081 849 9925
www.trimodestudio.com
Showroom open by appointment

V
Vanilla Garden 062
53 Ekkamai Soi 12
Sukhumvit Soi 63
T 02 381 6120
www.vanillaindustry.com
Vertigo and Moon Bar 065
Banyan Tree
21/100 Thanon Sathorn Tai
T 02 679 1200
www.banyantree.com

Vesper 048
*10/15 Thanon Convent
T 02 235 2777
www.vesperbar.co*

W
Wat Arun 045
*34 Thanon Arun Amarin
T 02 891 2185
www.watarun.org*
Wat Pho 009
*2 Thanon Sanamchai
Thanon Chetuphon*
WTF Gallery & Café 068
*7 Sukhumvit Soi 51
T 02 662 6246
www.wtfbangkok.com*

Y
Yarnnakarn 088
*2 Thanon Kamphaeng Phet
T 099 152 4635*
YenakArt Villa 073
*69 Soi Prasat Suk
Thanon Yen Akat
T 02 671 9413
www.yenakartvilla.com*

HOTELS
ADDRESSES AND ROOM RATES

Anantara Resort & Spa 096
Room rates:
double, from THB3,200
43/1 Thanon Phetkasem Beach
Hua Hin
T 03 252 0250
www.huahin.anantara.com

Arun Residence 022
Room rates:
double, from THB3,500;
Arun Suite, from THB5,800
36-38 Soi Pratoo Nok Yoong
Thanon Maharat
T 02 221 9158
www.arunresidence.com

The Cabochon Hotel 026
Room rates:
double, from THB5,300;
suite, from THB7,500
14/29 Sukhumvit Soi 45
T 02 259 2871
www.cabochonhotel.com

Casa de la Flora 100
Room rates:
villa, from THB18,000;
Presidential Suite, from THB31,500
67/213 Moo 5
Khuk Khak
Khao Lak
Phang Nga
T 07 642 8999
www.casadelaflora.com

Chakrabongse Villas 030
Room rates:
double, from THB5,800;
Garden Suite, THB9,000;
Thai House, THB11,200;
Riverside Villa, THB14,700;
Chinese Suite, THB26,000
396 Thanon Maharat
T 02 222 1290
www.chakrabongsevillas.com

The Beach Samui 097
Room rates:
suite, from THB9,800
30/23 Moo 5
Thong Krut Village
Tambon Taling Ngam
Koh Samui
T 07 723 4567
www.thebeach-samui.com

The Edition 016
Room rates:
prices on request
MahaNakhon Building
114 Thanon Narathiwat
T 02 055 1414
www.editionhotels.com

Grand Hyatt 044
Room rates:
double, from THB6,350
494 Thanon Ploenchit
T 02 254 1234
www.bangkok.grand.hyatt.com

Iniala Beach House 100
Room rates:
villa, from THB59,000
40/14 Moo 6
Khok Kloi
Takuathung
Phang Nga
T 07 645 1456
www.iniala.com

The Library 097
Room rates:
studio, from THB9,100
14/1 Moo 2
Chaweng Beach
Bo Phut
Koh Samui
T 07 742 2767
www.thelibrary.co.th

LiT 017
Room rates:
double, from THB4,000
36/1 Soi Kasemsan
Thanon Rama I
T 02 612 3456
www.litbangkok.com

Luxx XL 016
Room rates:
double, from THB2,300
82/8 Soi Lang Suan
T 02 684 1111
www.luxxxl.com

Mandarin Oriental 016
Room rates:
double, from THB17,250
48 Charoen Krung Soi 38
T 02 659 9000
www.mandarinoriental.com/bangkok

Millennium Hilton 016
Room rates:
double, from THB4,000
123 Thanon Charoen Nakhon
T 02 442 2000
www3.hilton.com

Hotel Muse 016
Room rates:
double, from THB5,700
55/555 Soi Lang Suan
T 02 630 4000
www.hotelmusebangkok.com

Park Hyatt 016
Room rates:
double, from THB9,000
88 Thanon Witthayu
T 02 012 1234
bangkok.park.hyatt.com

The Peninsula 016
Room rates:
double, from THB6,400
333 Thanon Charoen Nakhon
T 02 020 2888
www.peninsula.com/bangkok

Sala Rattanakosin 018
Room rates:
double, from THB3,800;
River View Deluxe, from THB6,200
39 Thanon Maharat
T 02 622 1388
www.salaresorts.com/rattanakosin

Shangri-La Hotel 031
Room rates:
double, from THB6,500;
Speciality Suite, THB110,000
89 Soi Wat Suan Plu
T 02 236 7777
www.shangri-la.com/bangkok

The Siam 024
Room rates:
suite, from THB18,000
3/2 Thanon Khao
T 02 206 6999
www.thesiamhotel.com

Siam Kempinski Hotel 027
Room rates:
double, from THB15,000;
Garden Suite, from THB24,000
991/9 Thanon Rama I
T 02 162 9000
www.kempinski.com/bangkok

Six Senses Yao Noi 103
Room rates:
villa, from THB20,800
56 Moo 5
Tambol Koh Yao Noi
Amphur Koh Yao
Phang Nga
T 07 641 8500
www.sixsenses.com

SO Sofitel 028
Room rates:
double, from THB6,800;
Water Rooms, from THB7,800;
Wood Rooms, from THB13,800
2 Thanon Sathorn Nua
T 02 624 0000
www.sofitel.com

X2 Kui Buri 102
Room rates:
villa, from THB4,500;
Luxury Pool Villa, from TBH15,000
52 Moo 13
Aoi Noi
Muang
Prachuap Khiri Khan
Kui Buri
T 03 251 0466
www.x2lobby.com

Yim Huai Khwang 020
Room rates:
Double Bed Garden, from THB1,650
70 Thanon Pracha Rat Bamphen
Huai Khwang
T 080 965 9994
www.yimbangkok.com

WALLPAPER* CITY GUIDES

Executive Editor
Jeremy Case

Author
Duncan Forgan

Deputy Editor
Belle Place

Photography Editor
Rebecca Moldenhauer

Junior Art Editor
Jade R Arroyo

Editorial Assistant
Charlie Monaghan

Contributors
Richard Mcleish
Adam Renton
Arglit Boonyai
Rob McKeown

Interns
Susan Le
Nicole Alber
Kathryn Younger

Production Controller
Nick Seston

Marketing & Bespoke Projects Manager
Nabil Butt

Wallpaper*® is a registered trademark of Time Inc (UK)

First published 2006
Fifth edition 2017

© Phaidon Press Limited

All prices and venue information are correct at time of going to press, but are subject to change.

Original Design
Loran Stosskopf
Map Illustrator
Russell Bell

Contacts
wcg@phaidon.com
@wallpaperguides

More City Guides
www.phaidon.com/travel

Phaidon Press Limited
Regent's Wharf
All Saints Street
London N1 9PA

Phaidon Press Inc
65 Bleecker Street
New York, NY 10012

Phaidon® is a registered trademark of Phaidon Press Limited

www.phaidon.com

A CIP Catalogue record for this book is available from the British Library.

All rights reserved. No part of this publication may be reproduced, stored in a retrieval system or transmitted, in any form or by any means, electronic, mechanical, photocopying, recording or otherwise, without the prior permission of Phaidon Press.

Printed in China

ISBN 978 0 7148 7379 4

PHOTOGRAPHERS

Christopher Wise
Bangkok city view,
inside front cover
MahaNakhon Tower, p012
Central Embassy, p013
LiT, p017
Sala Rattanakosin,
pp018-019
The Cabochon Hotel, p026
SO Sofitel, pp028-029
Ink & Lion Café, p033
RMA Institute, pp034-035
Almeta, p036
Bangkok Art and
Culture Centre, p037
Grand Postal Building,
pp038-039
The Never Ending Summer,
pp040-041
Museum of Contemporary
Art, p042, p043
Erawan Tea Room, p044
Bunker, p046, p047
Storyline, pp050-051
Osha, p052
Teens of Thailand, p053
Café Now by Propaganda,
p056

Tep Bar, p057
Quince, pp058-059
Bamboo Chic Bar, p060
Vanilla Garden, pp062-063
WTF Gallery & Café, p068
Soul Food Mahanakorn,
p069
Au Ekbutr Udomphol, p071
YenakArt Villa, p073
P Tendercool, p074
H Gallery, p078
100 Tonson Gallery, p079
Siri Apartment Building,
p084
The Met, p086
Atta Gallery, p092
56th Studio, p093

Alex Hill
Arun Residence,
pp022-023
Wat Arun, p045
Bo.lan, p061
Sirocco, p065
Robot Building, p085

Jason Michael Lang
Siam Kempinski Hotel,
p027
Nahm, pp066-067

Robert Polidori
CAT Building, pp010-011
Shangri-La Hotel, p031
Elephant Tower, pp014-015
Dusit Thani, p087

Marc Schultz
Chakrabongse Villas, p030
Salt, p064
X2 Kui Buri, p102

Wison Tungthunya
Casa de la Flora, p100,
p101

Ketsiree Wongwan
Islamic Centre of Thailand,
pp082-083

Getty Images
Suvarnabhumi Airport,
p081

BANGKOK
A COLOUR-CODED GUIDE TO THE HOT 'HOODS

CHATUCHAK
There's more here than a market, especially at night. Stop off on the way back from MOCA

OLD TOWN/BANGLAMPHU
Chinatown meets luxury hotel development along the bank of the fascinating Chao Phraya

SUKHUMVIT
It's all about the action-packed side streets that lead off this traffic-heavy thoroughfare

RATCHAPRASONG
A study of shopping contrasts, from slick malls on one side to neon-lit alleys on the other

SILOM/SATHORN
There are plenty of distractions in the city's financial heart, including many fine-diners

ARI
Bangkok's latest urban hotspot comprises a maze of leafy lanes lined with hip hangouts

For a full description of each neighbourhood, see the Introduction.
Featured venues are colour-coded, according to the district in which they are located.